NOT ALL BEER AND
SKITTLES

Commander Tom Foden

First Edition

ISBN number 0-9533249-0-7

Printed by J.W. Arrowsmith Ltd
Bristol BS3 2NT

 Petmac Publications
Bristol BS9 1QD
www.petmac.co.uk

PROLOGUE

During a Birthday Party in February 2000 I met Paul Blackham. Our conversation got around to my experiences in the Royal Navy and while serving with foreign navies, as a result of which Paul became determined that my memories should become available to a wider audience. We were joined shortly afterwards by Paul's daughter, Julia Whitaker, who brought professional writing skills to the enterprise. Much work by them both has resulted in this book.

I am very grateful for their assistance and perseverance.

I hope you will find as much pleasure in reading these memoirs as I have had in recalling them.

Tom Foden

*

I wrote Tom Foden's story by tape-recording his reminiscences and then converting them into print. They are set out in chronological form, as most autobiographies are.

In true Tom Foden style, during this process he understated a remarkable life in which he was deeply involved in the Second World War, served in two foreign navies and later was a driving force in the running of two renowned pleasure ships. The book recounts many strange situations, some sadnesses and atrocities but also a lot of light-hearted moments.

It has been a pleasure to have been allowed to share some of these experiences with a real gentleman, and with you.

Julia Whitaker

FOREWORD

by Sir Robert Wall, D Eng (h.c.), OBE, FCIT

Writer and lecturer on maritime affairs

Travellers who use the excursion services provided on the Bristol Channel by Waverley Excursions Limited have long become familiar with the amiable figure of Commander Tom Foden. For over a quarter of a century he has gone about the business of being Bristol Channel Agent and doing all that that demanding post requires. At any time of the day or night, Tom's skill, tact, authority, courtesy and wisdom can be called upon as the company goes about the business of preserving shipping excursion cruises around the coasts of Britain. Anything from booking tugs to organising charters is all in the routine of the job and has made Tom Foden well liked and widely respected by the maritime community that works and lives on the shores of the Bristol Channel.

Now Tom has, in this book, put on the record the full scope of his career at sea which has been long and covers some of this country's most fateful years of maritime history. Beginning in the great days of Empire and Tom's cadetship with P & O. it is a stirring tale of the Battle of the Atlantic and survival from sinking, convoys to besieged Malta and the great invasion operations of World War II – Torch and Overlord. After the War, came service with NATO and the Ghanaian and Imperial Ethiopian Navies, the latter bringing memories of the late Haile Selassie!

Tom Foden's story is full of interest, courage and good humour. It will appeal not only to those who 'go down to the sea in ships and have their business in great waters' but also to those many people who consider ships and the sea to be their natural heritage.

I heartily commend it.

Robert Wall

Chapter 1
Setting the Course
September 1914 to February 1939

Tom Foden was born in Bristol on 24th September 1914. His mother was connected with a well-known local family, part of the Lewis & Edbrooke Company, a building enterprise that had a history of construction work concerned with some of the great establishments in the City of Bristol; the Bristol Grammar School, Clifton College Chapel and the Avonside Engine Works (built at the turn of the 20th Century) to name but a few.

His mother, Marie, gave birth at home. Tom weighing around 10 pounds, was christened Thomas Howarth and was the first child and only son. The family doctor, Colston Wintle was present but his father, who was a Territorial in the Royal Gloucestershire Hussars, was unable to be there. At the time, the beginning of the First World War, most of the sergeants in the Territorial Army were taken to East Anglia to a training camp to be commissioned, but he was able to come home within the first couple of days to see his family.

One of the earliest memories Tom has of his father is of him telling him about the Foden Motor Works, of which he was a part. They had a very famous brass band and Tom says how proud he felt when listening to them, remembering all that his father had told him about them. By coincidence the band, many years later, went off to Egypt on tour when Tom was serving in the ship they sailed in. He remembers his father as a real character, someone who made a lot of "deals" for a living.

The family continued to live in Henbury until Tom was five years old. then they moved to Stoke Lane, Westbury-on- Trym.

He attended the Downs School, Upper Belgrave Road, and after that Glenmore School at Portishead. His mother was always concerned that he should be close to the sea, thinking that the air would do him good; not that he was a particularly sickly child. Little did she know then that Tom would have a life-long connection with the sea! Tom schooled in Portishead until he was 14, then attended Wellington School in Somerset.

Tom's school days at Wellington were not without their incidents, as he explains:

'One of my more painful, but amusing, recollections of life at Wellington School is the time that the Ist XI visited a well known West Country Catholic public school to play them at cricket. I was not in the First XI, I think I must have been scoring or something, to have been included at that particular match. Anyway, our team was almost unknown and we ended up beating them. To show how sporting their side could be, the cricket coach offered to meet us at 'The Castle of Comfort' pub, which was on our return journey, and stand us all a drink. Well, of course, we were delighted and the master who was with us, reluctantly and eventually, agreed to the break in our journey. We arrived at the pub to be offered a pint of sweet or dry draught cider. You can imagine the result! A couple of the boys made an awful mess in the coach and we were all in a dreadful state by the time we returned to school. Our particular Housemaster, I was in Darks house, took one look at us chaps in his section and ordered us all to report to his study immediately. In alphabetical order, we each received six of the best. Fortunately for me, he was tiring a little by the time he reached 'F' for Foden! But I for one decided it was not worth consuming alcohol under such conditions!'

Tom has other background memories of life at Wellington School:

'All schools have good and bad masters. We had a crowd of 'above average' really. There was one, however, who for a while was somewhat easygoing. I can't remember what subject he taught, but we had a lot of fun at his expense. It was around the latter part of 1929 and not all areas of the school buildings had central heating by then. Those parts without it had large, solid fuel stoves which were lit in the morning and then we had to keep them going after that. Well, we were taught twice a week, the period before lunch, by this particular easy-going master. A new solid type of methylated spirit tablet, a small white bar that looked like a throat lozenge, had been introduced to the camping fraternity for use on their cooking stoves. As a result of carrying out unauthorised experiments in the Chemistry Lab, we discovered that if these tablets were placed on to a hot (but not red-hot) surface, they would disintegrate all over the place! You can guess the rest. We put a few of these 'lozenges' on the top of the stove five minutes before the master was due to teach us and the whole room looked as though a snowstorm was happening! I think he eventually got to know how we did it, but for a long time we were able to get away with our behaviour! Our fun lasted until, on one particular occasion, the Headmaster was showing an influential Eastern potentate over the school. The party arrived outside our classroom at a very embarrassing moment when the storm was in full flight and looking very spectacular. That was the end of the fun, and also led to a lot of soreness in Form Lower V! We were worried that as a result of our conduct the master might disappear from the scene, but he remained at the school and became a completely different person. He turned into a strict disciplinarian, due I feel in no small way, to these little incidents that we made him suffer.'

While at Wellington, Tom thought very highly of the Headmaster, a chap called George Corner. George had an educational background in Engineering, something which was to prove useful to Tom and a few other "enthusiasts." The Head allowed Tom to keep an old EW Douglas motorcycle at the School, which his father had kindly bought for him at the huge expense of £5. Tom worked very hard on that bike, getting it into a superb condition at the school's expense, really, using the workshops, spare time and bits and pieces that he could find. He didn't keep it for very long though, selling it for a tidy profit of £7! At this point, I think it is probably fair to mention that Tom did try to make a "quid or two" when it came to the business of selling his bikes, but that didn't necessarily always happen! There will be more stories later on, but suffice it to say, the last bike that he sold, which was a new one, most definitely didn't allow for a tidy profit.

Tom was very keen on the Officer Training Corps (OTC), reached the exalted rank of Lance-Corporal and thoroughly enjoyed shooting, which was put to good use during the Second World War. In fact, his whole life at Wellington seemed to revolve around the OTC. The summer camps that they held were great fun and he and his chums used to take the train from Wellington (there is no longer a railway station there) and travel all the way to Tidworth. To mark their journey they would fly loo paper as streamers through the carriage windows, much to the guard's annoyance. They worked hard and played hard in the OTC and needed a week's sleep when they returned home for their summer holidays. He remembered this part of his life when the First World War was being left well behind and the beginnings of the Second World War, at 18 years old, were just a figment of his imagination.

About this time, his mother had been pushing him to go into his grandfather's Estate Agency and Builder's business. He realised that he was far more interested in the sea, but was unsure of how he could carry on this interest without upsetting his mother. He had spent a good many hours at Avonmouth, scrounging trips on King's Ltd. tugs coming in and out, and he knew that he would enjoy being a bigger part of something connected with the water. He says he learnt more seamanship from scrounging trips off Captain Trott on the tug *Merimac* than anywhere else! However, as he told me, it was decided for him, that for the time being, he should have a more cosmopolitan approach to furthering his career in his grandfather's business. There was an excellent company that his family knew of called Healey and Baker and he soon found himself in London working in this Estate Agency and, as he recalls, 'the years simply slipped by.'

It was some time between 1935 and 1936 that Tom plucked up the courage to go down to the Peninsular & Oriental Steam Navigation Company (P & O) offices in Leadenhall Street in London. Over a long luncheon with the correct and influential persona he decided that the P & O was definitely for him. He favoured this Organisation over the Royal Navy because he knew that he had left it really too late to enter the Navy as he was now 22 years of age, and ideally should have sought entry while in his teens, directly after leaving Wellington. Ironically, little did he know then that he would one day become part of the RN, but that will all become much clearer.

As Tom was not yet 25 years old when he was offered a position with the P & O the Appointing Officer required permission from his parents before he could join the organisation. He knew that this left him with rather a problem, especially where his mother was concerned. His determination was such that he went away and "fudged it", the approval that is, but as a result was accepted into their Supply and Secretariat Department. He could start almost straight away, 1 June! It was April then and he knew that he would have to break the news to his parents and the people he worked for.

Without thinking his way through these issues he handed in his notice to the senior partner at the Estate Agents, a chap called Baker. The consequences of this action were quite dire! Baker passed the information, almost immediately to Tom's mother. It seems this was only one of many "run ins" that Tom was to have with his family during his growing up! He was a young man of great character, even at this early stage in his development. He stood his ground and took the position offered and was located at Tilbury for his training period with P & O. The routine of living aboard whichever ship was in harbour was an excellent one. It showed the trainees a thing or two about what to expect of life at sea and the sort of tasks that they would have to carry out once their training was complete.

His early days there were not all plain sailing, but any worries were usually connected with his interest in motor-cycles rather than the training programme! Tom is a great collector. Besides an enthusiasm, in particular, for EW Douglas motorcycles, which were and always have been his favourite make, he also enjoyed motor cars. One of the earliest ones that he bought was a Morris Minor, a 1929 model. He bought this while at training school at Tilbury, but one day the back axle breathed its last and Tom ended up rooting around a scrap heap nearby for a replacement. Tom found a second-hand axle for 10 shillings and asked one of the Engine Room ratings, a Lascar called Harmar, to help him put the car back together. (Harmar used to clean the heads and do other odd jobs on board their training ship, *Comorin*.)

Anyway, they found some time one evening to work on this back axle, so that Tom would be able to go on leave that weekend. When they had replaced everything and tried the car out, putting it in gear, it went backwards! It was now about 10 o' clock at night, they were exasperated that they had put the crank wheel and pinion in back to front! It took them the rest of that night to make good their mistake, but such was their determination that Tom was able to go on leave that weekend. As you will discover, lots of these events went on in Tom's life and whenever they did he was able to ask for the support of other people along the way, when required. He had a lovely manner with people, an immense capacity for fun and people didn't mind helping him!

Training school was no problem to Tom but he had to have his Lifeboat Certificate of Competency before being allowed to go to sea. The P & O were very safety conscious and it was a great day when he joined *RMS Strathnaver*, in July 1937. He joined at Cadet status and didn't really know what he was doing; he had left it very late to go to sea and only six other cadets were allowed on board, including Brian Gordon Lyle Edwards, who shared a cabin with him. The Purser was HM The King's Private Secretary's brother, a gentleman called Meiville. So he set sail with quite a distinguished body of people.

Tom knew that news was pretty gloomy about the prospects of a war. On top of that, the work that he was doing seemed more concentrated than the Royal Navy cadets had to put up with. *Strathnaver* was running the Bombay Express Service and Tom liked the Purser; he thought that he was a good chap. This Purser rather befriended Tom and some of his chums on the second trip they made, and invited all the cadets to one of his drinks parties when they arrived in Bombay. Extraordinarily enough, Tom met a man called Brown at the cocktail party who was working in Bombay for the Hong Kong Shanghai Banking Corporation (HSBC, as it is more commonly known). Well, this chap was an Old Boy of Wellington School. He met Brown often after that and went up to his "super pad" in Bombay for a meal now and again. Neither of them knew it then, but during the war, Brown, who was a

Royal Navy Volunteer Reserve Officer became the Secretary to the Flag Officer, Bombay, and during the court-martial of Captain Hamer of *Bulolo* Brown was a real friend to Tom. However, that part of Tom's life comes later in the book.

After a spell on the *RMS Strathnaver*, Tom went to work ashore at the P & O Headquarters at Cockspur Street. It was during this period that one such encounter with a car, an 'M' type MG with a 4 speed gearbox to be precise, which he had bought for £12 and 10 shillings, revolutionised his social life. He was beginning to really find his feet with cars, bikes and girls!

He was not long ashore when he was commissioned to *RMS Stratheden*, the Flagship of the Fleet and a beautiful ship as Tom recalls. He also remembers that he had a super captain that he had the good fortune to work for, Commodore Sir Richard Harrison. Commander Tim Highley was the Purser. Tom got on well with both these senior officers and, on occasions acted as the Commodore's Secretary. This contact proved very useful to Tom, a few years, during the war. The Commodore often assisted the immediate boss (Harold H Fiddler) during the war years when it came to appointing people. Fiddler was a civilian from the Royal Mail Lines but was not as generous as the Commodore, who was available in his Headquarters in Richmond Park and one could always reckon on a good lunch there!

So, life on board *RMS Stratheden* was fun and also jolly hard work, with Tom burning the candle at both ends. The P & O operated their own Medical Service and Surgeon Commander Corbett was the Senior Medical Officer (SMO) on *Stratheden*. Corbett came to play squash with Tom one day and the very next day he asked to see Tom and told him that he had been working too hard and should take two or three weeks sick leave. The SMO even suggested that Tom might require more time off, after the initial leave was taken. Tom retells this with some mischief in his voice; it seems that Corbett and he became good friends. One may never know if there was a little bit of conspiracy going on there so that Tom could have an extended break, but he had worked very hard and deserved some leave anyway.

When he came back off this sick absence, he was appointed to that famous ship, *RMS Rawalpindi*. Unfortunately, she became better known for her tragic end at the hands of the German cruisers *Sharnhorst* and *Gneisenau*, than for her efforts in routine service.

At the end of one of the more auspicious trips that the ship made Tom remembers a small incident at the Dock gate in connection with, not unexpectedly, an MG vehicle. The car was an old one and his sister, Loveday, used to drive it home for him when he went aboard ship. The car did not have much in the way of brakes and therein lies the story.

It appears that Tom had to go to the bank to get the wages - £20,000, a lot of money by anyone's standards - and on entering the with the wages in tow a lorry coming up behind him could not stop; the lorry had even less in the way of brakes than his vehicle. The lorry driver gave Tom £20 for the trouble caused after they assessed the damage to Tom's car!

Neville Chamberlain went to see Hitler and as a result of their meeting war was delayed for a while longer. However, when they went outward bound the very next time, in September 1938 they were on the Japanese run. There were all sorts of stories about the threat of war. P & O Officers could now volunteer for the Royal Navy Reserve (RNR). A large number did but those that did not were more often than not ostracised by their P & O Officer colleagues. At the outbreak of war, those officers who were in the RNR were then called up for war service, changing their uniforms from P & O to RNR.

Activity started to convert the ships; gun bases were fitted immediately on *RMS Rawalpindi*, 'just in case' war broke out, and guns were embarked out of sight of the passengers. In fact, the ship was made ready as an Armed Merchant Cruiser. A lot of Tom's time, with some other chaps, was spent fitting the bases for these guns and it was only when they reached Gibraltar that the situation seemed to be better and the possibility of war still appeared to be some distance away. Captain Draper, RNR, who was commanding this great ship was not so sure that everything really was all right so he instructed them all to leave everything in position and to be ready to hoist the guns up from the hold if required at short notice. The threat of war, however, was not without its distractions and Tom's memory serves him well for this particular voyage:

'Lovely voyage, two charming girls from Roedean School in Brighton going back to their dads in Hong Kong for the summer holidays joined us and then we went on to Japan.'

He recalls this with a small amount of affection in his voice. He felt quite rich at the time and bought an old EW Douglas motorcycle. One of his chums had an old Enfield and somehow they managed to land these in Japan. The police there were told that Tom and his mate held International Driving Licences and so they were allowed to go out on the roads. Tom laughs when he told me how atrocious the roads really were, so much so that one chap broke his leg one night. With the threat of war looming the Japanese were unhelpful; no ambulance appeared and he and two chums had to take the victim to the Mission to Seaman hostel instead.

Tom is proud to say that he is associated with this great institution and on that particular occasion the Mission did a great job and patched his chum up. He was certain that if the matter had been left to the police and the Japanese, then they would probably have left him there!

This was the penultimate sailing before *RMS Rawalpindi* became a Royal Navy ship. Luckily for Tom, they returned to Hong Kong on the way back and picked up the same Roedean ladies again, making it a very happy return voyage indeed. Crossing the Bay of Biscay they experienced some atrocious weather. If the weather is good in the Bay it can be great, but this must have been one of the worst days in December of 1938.

Matters were made worse because of the unfortunate arrival on board of a certain lady picked up in Colombo, Ceylon (Sri Lanka). It appears that she was some 'old mother judge', as Tom puts it, an Indian lady who thought she could foretell the future; she gave some terrible advice, spreading tales that the world would end on the 20th December. Unfortunately for all concerned on the ship it was the 20th December when they were in the Bay, and some of the passengers believed her! Tom and a handful of the other officers tried to placate these people but it was a really bad time, so much so that they had to alter course because the ship was rolling so badly. Tom remembers:

'The temporary course was shown on a blackboard. In really appalling weather the ship was steered manually. The weather was so bad on this particular voyage that even the blackboard fell off the bulkhead. This meant that when the helmsman was relieved after his two-hour watch, the new helmsman returned the ship to the True Course, which meant the ship rolled severely for a few minutes until the Officer of the Watch realised that the blackboard was lying on the deck! All's well that ends well as the saying goes, and the Officer on

Watch was able to make the ship steady on its right course in a safe and professional manner.

They arrived in the UK in early 1939, and in August of that year the cruiser then became *HMS Rawalpindi*. It was taken over by Naval personnel, Tom was sent on leave and that was the end of his days with the P & O. There was so much ahead for him then, but at the time, had he known what was in store, he would have been sad to think that his sailing days with the P & O were over.

Anyway, back to the motorcycles. Tom had to put soap around the petrol tank to stop the leaks. Of course, this meant that you had to use the petrol, otherwise it would just disappear. As already mentioned, very fortunately, the Headmaster at Wellington School, George Corner, was also interested in motorcycles and used to help some of the boys. This revolutionised many of the bikes.

Tom's kept his EW Douglas for quite a while after he left Wellington and eventually swapped it with a chum, buying an Ivory Calthorpe from Kings of Oxford. There was a succession of bikes as he became fed up with one or other purchase. He changed the Ivory Cathorpe for a Royal Enfield 2-Stroke which, why I am not sure, was a disaster. Tom says it did not have any brakes, and recalls going down Maudlin Street in Bristol on it once and having to brake for a tram. This was impossible, as the harder he braked, the better it went! Tom had to put the motorcycle in bottom gear and jump up on the pavement to stop it! Obviously it had to go, quickly being replaced by a Francis Barnett 172cc TT Super Sports.

Tom was only 17 years old then and took this bike up to London now and then. Usually this happened when he was given money by close members of the family, his mother or grandparents. It was good for him, since he got to see more of his father, who now lived in London because his parents had separated.

There is a determination in Tom's voice when he talks specifically about EW Douglas bikes, though. He says they were the stuff that bikes were made of, and I think they will always be his favourite. The last model of the EW Douglas was made in 1928 and he, of course, owned one. He kept it for nearly a year! This seemed a long time to Tom, with the frequency with which he swapped his motorcycles, but on all of them his girlfriends were proudly borne. I think the fact that this particular model, the EW Douglas never let him down when he had a girl on the back to impress was part of his empathy with the design!

He was now working at his grandfather's business. Like all boys with toys, though, he kept thinking that he really wanted a 600cc Douglas bike, as they were all the rage at the time. Having found one advertised by Kings of Leicester for £16, Tom was sorely tempted to part with his savings in order to buy it.

The end of the working day on the Friday at the end of March saw Tom travelling to Leicester on his Douglas, so that he could take a look at the 600 bike. It was a lovely day, and he travelled through the beautiful Cotswolds with his bike going very well. The Kings of Leicester chap was not very happy to see Tom, however, because he hadn't had time to overhaul the 600. And to add insult to injury the model was a 1929 version, where Tom had thought it was a 1930 design. But having come so far that he was determined to go away with it, whatever the condition! The chaps at Kings weren't even sure that the motorcycle was up to a 100 mile journey, the first problem being a flat battery. Anyway, it was about 4 o'clock in the afternoon, the formalities were finished and Tom even knocked them down a bit on the asking price.

Tom got through to Warwick without any mishaps, it was dark then, early evening, about 6 o'clock. He had confidence in the bike, the lights were working properly because they worked directly from the dynamo, so if the engine was working, then they were, too. All too soon, however, there was a terrible noise around the back wheel and the whole of the chain-sprocket and some spokes came loose. Luckily for him, he had passed a pub about a mile back; Tom pushed the bike all the way, arriving at about 9.30 in the evening. He was very glad that the landlord had a room to give him for the night, although it cost him 10 bob.

Tom was realising that this bike was turning out to be very expensive, and it was very early days with it as well. He stayed until the next morning, but of course had to locate some new parts. After many phone calls and much expense, he managed to find what it was he was after in London.

I think that you will agree that he had a greater level of determination than most when you hear that he then had to get on a Royal Blue coach to London in order to pick up another wheel and tyre. Perhaps, later, he saw it as good growing-up material, but at the time all it seemed to be was a necessity, so that he could get his bike back on the road. He caught another Royal Blue coach back to the pub, stayed another night, and then on the Sunday took his bike to a local garage so that they could get it going for him.

Tom's understatements throughout these events is unbelievable. His very next statement is the one I love the most, and became the title for the book: 'It wasn't all beer and skittles you know!'

The story continues with the realisation that the weather was getting worse, he was travelling through Moreton-in-Marsh in the dark and the further he went the more the weather deteriorated. Because of the rain, the major roads were frozen like sheets of glass and it made it a very unpleasant journey indeed. To top it all, when he arrived home his mother was not best pleased with him and he spent the whole of the next day recovering from the experience.

From beginning to end, this bike was a disaster. In no time at all the kick-start broke, the sprocket inside the gearbox went and Tom couldn't even get one from the factory. To cap it all, the bike had to be pushed for the rest of its life every time he wanted to start it. Tom's stepfather gave him some good advice, 'flog it, and quick', but before he had a chance to do this there was worse to come.

Tom was in Bristol one evening drinking with some mates, along with another chum of his who lived opposite him. Well, someone in a car came out of George Street and blocked Park Street; Tom and the motorcycle almost finished up under a bus and the bike caught fire. It seems that luck follows Tom around and he got off with just a few bruises and scratches. Everyone was told to keep clear and the bus proceeded on its way. At the top of Park Street there was a Riley agency, who took the wreck off Tom and put it in their garage. When he arrived home he was met with a very strange welcome. Someone had called his mother to say that Tom was dead and she didn't know whether to be furious or relieved. His stepfather got rid of the bike for him - but not for long. Tom found out where he had taken it and went and bought it back from them and put it in the Conservatory! One of Tom's chums, Bruce Douglas (the grandson of William Douglas who was the founder of the motorcycle manufacturers in Bristol) took a look at the frame. They both decided that he needed a new one and Bruce promised to find one for Tom. Being in the business, so to speak, Bruce was able to kit out Tom's old frame and other parts from the production line, swapping the old parts for new. This practice was carried out so that no-one could see that anything was missing from any of the bikes on the line. This, of course, meant that someone else's new bike actually had some of Tom's old bits on it! They built up the wreck of the bike and Tom's stepfather found some chaps in Bedminster who gave £25 for it. A new version of the bike then cost only about £60!

During the time that Tom had the 600cc Douglas he bought a sidecar for it. His main reason for doing so was that he had a great girlfriend in Solihull, and thought that if he had a more comfortable attachment to the bike she might come down to one of the dances he enjoyed going to in Bristol. Tom sought the advice of the brother of this girlfriend, Joan, but he rather put him off, saying that she wouldn't want to come out in it. So Tom didn't pursue that one, but he got the sidecar anyway! This, too, was going to be a short lived experience, as you will see.

The next weekend Tom and a chum of his, along with prominent members of the Knowle and District MCC, the Bristol Motor Club and the Douglas Club decided to run a 'jaunt' to Lynmouth. His friend was a chap called Williams, who owned a lovely new 600cc Douglas, a beautiful thing as Tom recalls, but Williams couldn't use his legs and had had this bike specially adapted for him. The Douglas Company made him a new bike every year at some expense to Williams, however, there was something wrong with it at that time, so that was why they took the sidecar. Not that Tom minded, he rather wanted to give it a good try out.

Neither of them were certain if they would be able to get up Porlock Hill! Alas, it seemed that they were not meant to do so; the more the clutch slipped, the more they realised they would be unsuccessful. What a sight it must have been, Williams on his crutches with Tom alongside pushing the bike and sidecar all the way up Porlock Hill on one side and then having additional worries about going down the other. Apart from controlling it, Tom knew that the brakes were very dodgy, so it was a real nightmare. It was the only time that Tom ever had anything to do with sidecars on motorbikes! He sold it to a chum, who did very well with it!

Tom recounts another time when he still had this sidecar. He was travelling down Whiteladies Road, lost control and somehow managed to get the bike and sidecar wedged between one of the lamp standards in the road! Apart from getting a terrible shock, he was none the worse for the experience. Again, at Boyce's Avenue, Clifton, attempting to turn from Regent Street into Boyce's Avenue, he forgot that he had a sidecar attached! It went up in the air and to get it down again he had to accelerate on the corner and travel up the pavement, ending up nudging Marsh's shop window in order to bring it down again! Remarkably, he only scraped it and took a little bit off the woodwork of the shop window. It was a bit touch and go for a while, as the situation unfolded.

Tom had also got to know another man by then who's father was the Managing Director of the Douglas enterprise, Bobby Millman. He had a 1932 Light 500cc Douglas for sale for £25, a lovely, chromium bike, really super. Luckily for him, Bobby's sister didn't like it and so he decided to sell it. According to Tom this bike did everything. It was so light that he had to be a bit careful on it: 'It was so fast that the front wheel would come off the ground!'

Very exciting times! He kept it for a long time and talks as if he wished that he still had it. It was one of the bikes that he took to sea with him. He then bought a Matchless, but didn't like it much. He took part in a few standard tyre trials with it, but never did very well. He also took it on a couple of grass-track races, popular at the time.

The affection for one particular model must be fickle, for he then bought a brand-new AJS-BHY 905. 'That was really good, just about the same as the Light 500 Douglas, but it was only a 250 cc, very nippy and I had a lot of fun with it.'

On one occasion, he took a girlfriend on the back and they enjoyed the ride together, ending up at a pub in New Passage for a pint of cider. After the drink they set off back to Bristol, but, sadly he was rather the 'worse for wear.' For those of you who are not old enough to know this, traffic lights had just been brought in! They were red, Tom couldn't sit on the bike, he kept falling off. Unfortunately, when the lights went green, this girl had to get him on the bike and start it up! Tom becomes very serious at this point; 'really sorted me out to not drink and drive.' Of course, his mother was hopping mad again and his life was made very hard for a while. Tom says that it put him off bikes for a time. But he then bought a 'D' type MG on hire purchase, found it hard getting used to the car and, besides, couldn't afford the payments.

There are plenty of incidents, here and there, concerning a bike, a car, a chum or one luscious girl or another, which all made up part of a wonderful life. Tom is, and always has been, a very colourful and endearing person and throughout this book, you will see that people helped him when he was in tight corners or in need of a helping hand. He, in turn, although he plays matters down, was dependable and a good chum to many people during his life.

I would like you to join me in the journey through the remarkable memories that Tom has found the time to tell. It is no wonder that he has been offered some very interesting jobs in some very out-of-the-way places. Many of these jobs could only be done by someone with the qualities that Tom shows.

Before leaving this chapter, Tom would like to say:

'I think you can see that I was a bit of a tearaway. However, I would like to say what a wonderful experience Wellington School was. I hated my first couple of terms but there is no way one can equal the character formation experience of a good public school. I joined as a rather superior little boy and left as a man. The formative years from 14 - 17 are so important, it proved the best investment my parents ever made.'

Chapter 2
Torpedoed by a Gentleman
March 1939 to July 1941

On leaving the P & O, just as the Second World War was beginning, Tom knew that everybody on board was all ready, "guns up, raring to go", so to speak. However, it seemed that the Admiralty had other ideas; some of the crew were sent on leave and others remained on board and crew replacements were made with RNVR chaps who had very little experience. So from March 1939 onwards Tom and the RNR men were just waiting to see what was going to happen when they were sent on leave. Tom explains:

'Before the war, your initial two weeks training in the RNR was in *HMS Iron Duke*, an old iron battleship in Portsmouth. As a gunnery training ship, she had been de-militarised, but was the original Super-Dreadnought which had served as the flagship of Commander-in-Chief, Sir John Jellicoe in the First World War, taking part in the only major naval engagement of the war, the indecisive Battle of Jutland. It gave a perfectly good idea of life in the Navy. You spent a few days in Gunnery or whatever else you were going to specialise in. There was a saying used on these chaps, 'the RNR were sailors trying to be gents and the RNVR was the other way round.'

Tom suggests that those that had been in the P & O were fairly good at being on the gentleman side too!

'I came back to Bristol, just as war was starting, I drove down in an MG 'M' type I had picked up for £15. I stayed with Mum and my stepfather in the flat at Queen's court in Bristol. One day followed another, I became quite nonchalant about what was going on really, either the Royal Navy or the P & O were paying me then, I can't remember which.'

The days seemed to follow each other, in some form of oblivion. Tom wandered around Bristol Docks, where he saw an old Egyptian Freighter, the *Memphis*, the Captain of which frequented the same pub as he did. Tom starts his story, remembering an encounter in the pub:

'The Captain asked me if I wanted a job for a week or two, he would sign me on for a few weeks, but if a signal came I would be in trouble. Fortunately, I didn't take him up on the offer and a good job too, for I received a signal to join *HMS Mersey* and was immediately put on a course to show how people were paid and how the administrative side of the Navy worked.'

About that time, Tom got to know a nice girl with an Austin 7 who came from Portishead, but he had met her in Liverpool. Rather wistfully, Tom reminisces:

'Peggy Heaven was her name and the song was Ginger Rogers' 'Heaven, I'm In Heaven.' The chaps used to sing it whenever we were seen in the Wardroom together.'

Tom couldn't take his car up to Glasgow, so he went by train, remembering it as an awful journey. He had to change at Crewe and while there all these experienced people kept saluting him and eventually he arrived at Greenoch, well after nightfall. He recalls how he:

'Got some smoky old Drifter, conveying liberty men from ships to shore and I returned on one of these trips to *HMS Salopian*. I very quickly realised that this was an old Bibby Line ship (*MV Shropshire*) which was used on their express service from Liverpool to Rangoon. We kept a lot of the same personnel on board; they were good seamen but the P & O chaps did not have a lot in common with them. They used to treat us very badly, mimicked and teased us, but it was a good ship and I hope we did some good work with it.'

The first trip was well remembered, as were all the trips on *HMS Salopian* - I am sure you will see why by the end of this chapter. Tom says:

'We went off to sea as one of the Northern Patrol Ships, basically covering from the North of Scotland to the ice limit in the North, above Iceland. The ship used to look like something from a Father Christmas film. Ice in the rigging was one of the main problems. When this happened the ship became very unstable, it was just like being in a sailing ship, and we all had to go up in the rigging and break the ice down. There were one or two false alarms.'

Tom heard the news about *HMS Rawalpindi:* only a few survivors, it made him realise that a war was on.

'We came back at the end of 1940, beginning of 1941, it was Christmas time and sadly I was taken sick. We had a dear old surgeon called Freeman, Irish as can be, who told me I had pneumonia and would have to be put ashore' Tom chuckles, 'Just my luck, Christmas leave was coming up, but I had to take mine in a hospital at Newton Mearns in Glasgow as they could cure my illness with a new drug called penicillin! And they did and I soon got better, but all my leave had been taken up so I had to go straight back to the ship. I was very fed up.'

They did one or two more patrols and when they came back the Flag Officer, Northern Patrol, came on board to tell them that they had decided to take the ship off the Patrol and that they were to become part of a Convoy Escort group, with ships based on Halifax, Nova Scotia. Tom says that there was great secrecy concerning their patrols:

'This was told us in great secrecy. After the next Patrol we would be over in America and would be based on Halifax. So, knowing this, I told my mother, also in great secrecy. I even denuded my room at home of all my belongings so I could have them with me in my cabin. These treasures included, "The Conrod", Douglas 1925 magazine borrowed from the boss (Bobby Millman's father), pictures, a wireless and lots more.

'We were still on Northern Patrol in April, the weather was just getting warmer and we caught sight of what we thought was a 'pocket battleship', but it was a Norwegian Trawler and the Norwegians had only just entered into the war then, so no harm was done. The last Patrol was just completed, we went up to the ice gap, came back to Reykjavik and then went to Seydisfjordur and saw an American Destroyer!' Tom explains:

'This is one part of my career where my memory is a bit sketchy. In 1941, *Salopian* was well established on the Northern Patrol, with occasional 24-hour visits to Iceland, sometimes Reykjavik where, on one occasion, I visited the Borg Hotel and saw some of the lovely tall, Icelandic girls with their beautiful fair hair. We could not stay longer owing to the Neutrality rules. Sometimes, we refuelled in remote fjords, usually at night. On one such occasion, in Seydisfjordur, a modern and unusual Destroyer was also refuelling from the same Royal Fleet Auxiliary Vessel (hereafter called RFA). The Master-at-Arms staff were not encouraging the ship's company on to the Upper Deck. I took a closer look (well as close as was prudent) and to my amazement discovered the ship was a United States Navy Destroyer! It appeared that she had been very busy on Anti-Submarine duties in the area - with some success I might add. We asked no questions. The Americans entered the war some months later. By the time that *Salopian* was sunk, over six months later, Iceland had entered the war on our side.'

Tom returns to the Northern Patrol:

'Now, it was the end of April, but there was still a lot of snow lying about. People seemed pleased to see us, reassured to know that we were around.' Tom's ship went alongside other vessels, where he found that he had one or two chums on this ship *HMS Salopian*.

'I was a Supply Officer, and the Senior Supply Officer was also from the P & O, with whom I had served in *RMS Rawalpindi*, a chap called Don Sinclair. We both thought that we should get some old crock of a car if we were going to stay in Halifax and luckily enough we were offered one for $50. We ended up with some old two-seater Chrysler between us, it was a big car, it drank petrol and went well, generally and made life more pleasant.'

The ship ended up doing a few Patrols, nothing serious. It was about mid-May by then and again they found themselves with a couple of days leave to take. Certainly, after this time ashore, Tom remembers the sequence of events which changed the rest of his life, really.

He recounts:

'Things seemed to be bucking up, there were a few ships getting ready for the next Convoy, some Bristol City Line ships were there too, we were headed on a course which took us to 25 degrees West, that was as far as we went with the Convoy and then the responsibility was handed over to the local Escort. Luckily, we didn't meet anything, we heard more on the wireless and the dreadful news about *HMS Hood*, which had been blown up by the *Bismarck*. This didn't improve our morale at all. Anyway, we turned around and proceeded back to Halifax. When you leave a Convoy, you naturally have to report to the Admiralty the position where you are, exactly. I was on cipher watch at the time and had to cipher up the message and give it to the Senior Radio Officer. This Officer told me that the High Frequency Radio was on the blink, so the Signal would have to be sent by Medium Wave Frequency. I just couldn't believe this, every sub within 1000 miles would know where we were, I thought, but the Officer said he was sure that we could send the Signal quickly and it wouldn't be a problem. Our Captain, Captain Sir John Alleyn (he was a great seaman, but didn't know much about Radio communications, especially the modern side of things) had given the Chief Radio Officer authority to transmit on the Medium Frequency. Fatal.

'High Frequency transmitters, however, were very difficult to Direction Find and every ship was equipped with one, so I could not understand why we were not using ours. The 'old boy' didn't really know what was going on. I told my chums that I didn't like this and also informed the Commander of the situation that we might place ourselves in. He was more equipped with information on the Radio scene. Anyway, I had a lovely dinner, filled my coat pockets up with chocolate, turned in and kept my clothes on. Well, we were caught, 05.00 in the morning, there was a dreadful bang and we all went to "Action Stations." I could see from the manoeuvres that the Sub was not a fool; he closed in on us so that he was almost alongside, we just couldn't deflect the guns low enough to get to him. Anyhow, he spoke perfect English. "Sorry to torpedo you, we'll give you half an hour to get into your boats." Our Captain was furious.

'The U-boat Captain spoke again, "Let's behave like gentlemen," he said. "You now have fifteen minutes before we put in another torpedo." True to the second, the U-boat Captain gave us 15 minutes and we were then hit by another torpedo. *HMS Salopian* was a strong diesel ship, the torpedoes tracked our engines, all the injectors were broken. We had done nothing and said nothing, so the Sub Captain said again, "Sorry Captain, we will give you another 15 minutes." Well, we got the boats out and started lowering them, using Welling Quadrant Davits. The remaining personnel on board were the Captain, the Chief Radio Officer and a few others. There was no problem except that we were scared to death that we would take another torpedo.

'It took four torpedoes to sink that ship. It was a very strong ship, it was from the Bibby Line, as I said, the one on the Liverpool and Avonmouth service to Rangoon. The Navy used to fill these liners with barrels of air, knowing that they could float so well and it was unlikely that all the barrels would fall out if you were torpedoed. It took us two minutes to get launched. In the lifeboat there were two Officers, myself and Lieutenant Arthur Nance (who in peacetime was the Captain of the *Scilonian*, working between Penzance and the Scilly Isles) and also a total of thirty-four sailors made up of Chief Petty Officers (CPOs), Petty Officers (POs) and ratings. We got the oars away and stood by, well clear of the ship. There were six lifeboats in all. We were practically able to take everyone away in the boats, which was most unusual. We watched the events that unfolded next.

'When we were still on board, we had tried to send out a message to the Admiralty, the sailor responsible for tapping it out didn't think it was getting through, so another sailor went up the mast to stick up another aerial. A torpedo came along, took it down again, it was very unlikely that any message got out.'

Tom emphasises:

'The Captain of the U-boat was very, very correct. I later found out his name: Reverend Pastor Nemer Muller. He was a real gentleman, very different from the U-boat Captains we came across later in the war. He sank our ship and asked us if we wanted him to send a message, or if we needed a Doctor or any other assistance. Our Captain was not very helpful. The

Sub cruised around us and then left. The first thing that we did was to find out if the Senior Radio Officer had managed to send any communication. It was understood that we had got the message perfectly well off, but it was unlikely that any of the signals had gone anywhere, because of the aerials coming down. Even our lifeboat's generator was damaged, so the transmitter had to be wound round and round to make a spark to send the message, hoping that someone would be picking it up.'

'In fact, an independent merchant ship had picked it up, but had to pass on the message a day later, as they were maintaining radio silence. The U-boat also sent a message, saying that they had sunk a ship called the *Shropshire*! The Admiralty, who also received the message, realised who we were, though. The *MV Shropshire* was the original name of *HMS Salopian*, but as the original name had been embossed in steel and then painted over, the U-boat Captain read it and signalled the wrong name to his HQ. Lord Haw Haw announced this on the radio, that it was *HMS Shropshire!* The Admiralty then sent the destroyer, *HMS Impulsive* to the position received from the independent merchant ship, to look for survivors. The Admiralty asked for our position, course and speed to be reported immediately; it didn't come of course, so the destroyer *Impulsive* came from Reykjavik to see if they could find us. They arrived at the position where the U-boat had said he had sunk us.'

Tom explains conditions in the lifeboat:

'We were very lucky, we were left out there for five days. As you can imagine, we were getting pretty short of drinking water and the sailors cottoned on to the chocolate that I had, so they had some, too. It was on the fifth day, in the morning, we were all getting a bit despondent and if no ships had come by the sixth day, with the prevailing South Westerly winds, we knew that we would have to try to get to Reykjavik. Unfortunately, our rations were proving a problem. The sailors, being sailors, had nicked the food that had been stowed on the lifeboats to use for their rations on board, and so these lockers had been opened and were rather depleted! In the open boats, the weather was really quite good in the Western Ocean, there was decent weather in May, the sea was only Force 2 or 3 and a bit cold at night, but pretty near all of us had heavy weather gear on. We also had more sails than we needed and used them for protection at night. We were all terribly stiff but only one person died in the boats. The chap was wounded in the Engine room during one of the torpedo explosions. Other casualties from that U-boat attack were 14 in total. That was out of a company of 350, so that was very good really.'

Tom was asked how they had coped. His reply was:

'Water was difficult, we rationed ourselves to half a cup morning, lunch and night, but it was just not enough.'

It seems that luck was truly with them as Tom tells how they were rescued:

'The Captain's motorboat saw something on the horizon and the destroyer saw the rocket that we sent up as a result of that and by the grace of God, we were rescued. The destroyer only had enough fuel to search for about a further two hours or so, so we were just noticed in time. The Captain made a speech to the survivors when we came alongside the jetty in Reykjavik; we marched off like RN personnel. He said that we were all safe but we must now be ready to have another go, just as soon as we could join ships again.'

Tom goes on:

'The Brits had landed in Iceland and so we survivors went to an Army camp near Reykjavik and then returned to Clyde, Scotland in the *Royal Ulsterman.'*

As if Tom and his fellow crewmen had not suffered enough, the ship did everything but turn over because of the dreadful weather on that voyage back. They landed at Gourock and went their separate ways. Tom went home.

'I was given two weeks survivor's leave, with the possibility of four weeks on top of that. I went back to Queens court in Clifton, Bristol.'

Unfortunately for him, he found himself taking the train at Glasgow at 5.40 p.m. He says this particular train journey used to be known as the "Romance Express", but for him it certainly wasn't. The train travelled as far as Crewe where a troop train embodied itself with their train; this in turn, decided to terminate at Wolverhampton! Tom was informed that it would probably go on to Bristol. He says it was not a very easy journey anyway, as the trains were so intermittent. Well, this train went to Wolverhampton, unloaded the troops and then went into the sidings! Tom was stopped by the Home Guard and explained himself, took another train to Birmingham and gradually made his way to Bristol.

Tom wasn't terribly happy to go back as he had become engaged before leaving on his last trip and he was pretty sure that the lady in question would have made arrangements for an early marriage. Tom says:

'She would have heard Lord Haw Haw's news that *HMS Salopian* had been sunk, but I had not been posted as missing, so it was more than likely that I would turn up soon. Not only that, I was right! She had made all the arrangements for the wedding to go ahead in Bristol Cathedral and the banns had been called three times. My mother was horrified, but not as much as I was. Wedding presents were arriving as well!'

Poor Tom, what a fix. He arrived back to all this after such an adventurous trip, all round. That wasn't the end, however!

'On my first night back, I drove my car, an 'M' type, 4-speed gearbox MG which I had bought for 12 pounds and 10 shillings from home where it was garaged. What a thrill, this car had revolutionised my social life and was about to witness another change. On the way to collect my fiancée I called at the Royal Hotel in Portishead for a couple of drinks. When I picked her up, we drove to a pretty little lane, off the main road in Portbury, for a serious discourse. All I wanted was to put the wedding back a couple of weeks, especially after all I had been through. She tried to persuade me to proceed with the wedding. The discussion deteriorated into a flaming row, culminating in her removing her engagement ring, opening the car door and throwing the ring into the hedge! In the frosty atmosphere all I could do was to back the car down the lane, take her home and return to Queens court. Everyone was in bed when I arrived back, so I 'turned in' myself. The following morning, my mother brought me a cup of tea. I knew that my sister, Loveday, who was now married, was also staying there and I told her the story:

'Her reaction was wonderful, she said that we had a spare day on our hands and we should return to Portbury and recover the ring! I was really not so sure, in fact, my mind was in such a whirl after all the incidents of the last few weeks I didn't know what was going on. Anyway, Loveday made cheese sandwiches, filled a thermos with coffee, and armed with a trowel and a fork, off we went. We searched the area methodically, square by square, until about 3 o'clock in the afternoon. I was all for abandoning the task but my sister insisted that we continue until 5.00 o'clock, then we could give up. I would never have believed it, but within five minutes of re-starting the search, she found the ring! We were so overjoyed that on returning home we opened a bottle of white wine to celebrate the great discovery. I took the ring to

Mr Denbo, the Jeweller in Park Street, Bristol, who gave me £30 for it. It was a good deal of money and I almost felt like a millionaire!'

After this event, Tom went to his sister's in Bewdley, where she lived with her husband, John. The Admiralty let Tom have more time off and said he might end up at the Admiral's office in Liverpool. He says:

'So I stayed on at my sister's and I saw another MG 'M' type with a 4 speed gearbox for £5 at the local garage there. They suggested that the one I already had, and this one on offer, together, would make one good car. I bought the second MG and arranged to leave my original with it at Bewdley garage when I left the UK. Then, I was appointed to *HMS Mersey* at Liverpool, where I was asked to reconstruct the pay accounts from *HMS Salopian*.'

Tom explains that this is what you have to do if you are unable to take the pay documents off a ship that has been sunk.

'The Supply Officer and I were both up there at Liverpool from *HMS Salopian*, that is Don Sinclair and myself. We both had a lovely big cabin and a writer to assist with the *Salopian* Ship's Company accounts. Everyone received more or less the wages that they were due. *HMS Mersey* had increased a lot by then and Donald Wyatt, the Commodore's secretary, whom I got on with, told me that he was desperate for officers and he said he would ask the Admiralty if I could be appointed his assistant when *HMS Salopian's* work was completed. I understood that this would be for about 6 months. So I had a lovely time, there were lots of luscious WRENs, some of them were attached to the Admiral's office. I thought, 'looks good,' but few had real brains. I had managed to keep the old MG going until I left the UK, it was not going to be rebuilt until after I had returned to sea, so I was mobile while on land.'

*

Chapter 3
To Malta on HMS Breconshire
August 1941 to May 1942

Tom was then appointed to *HMS Breconshire*. He took great pains to find out that she was a Special Service ship which the Navy had requisitioned.

'She was a fast cargo ship built for Alfred Holt in Hong Kong. We took on some very nasty cargo to Malta as the Merchant Navy wasn't too keen, so I joined her in Glasgow, having dropped my car off. I returned to the King George V Docks in Glasgow, by train, having said "au revoir" to a new special girlfriend who lived in the flat above us in Queens court, Bristol.'

Tom said:

'I didn't enjoy the ship, about 130 people, nice lot, junior sub-lieutenant - loaded coal, petrol in tins, lots of bombs etc. I went into Glasgow one night and bought a Royal Enfield 250cc from Mr Bell and as our Captain liked motorcycles he let me keep it in the ship, and off we sailed. We went to the tail of the Bank, on the Clyde and waited for the Convoy: three or four Merchant Ships who were going with us to Malta. There was a Pacific Steam Navigation Company ship amongst them; these were very, very fast ships of the Blue Funnel Line, and one Clan Line ship, all hand-picked for this hazardous voyage. The tremendous escort also had *HMS Nelson* and the Aircraft Carrier *HMS Eagle* among them. There was enough to take the PM to America. Going to Gibraltar we had no problems, any submarine with any sense within fifty miles would leave us alone. When we arrived there, we picked up another six destroyers, and also an Anti-Aircraft Cruiser, *HMS Cairo.'*

Tom pauses for a short time, bringing back the scenes to him, just as if they were yesterday. He then continues:

'The first day was okay, but not the second. *HMS Nelson* was hit by German torpedo bombs, but she kept going. The Admiral transferred to one of the Aircraft Carriers and *Nelson* was ordered to return to Gibraltar with a couple of the destroyers, as Escort. The Admiral was definitely worried that we would run out of ammunition. The sky was full of aeroplanes, all Italians and Germans. Sadly, we lost one of the merchant ships and a couple of the destroyers, and *HMS Eagle* was badly damaged. They were determined to stop us but we were not to be put off. Several more hits found their mark, but not on us. Our Captain was a great seaman and somehow always prevented us from getting hit. He manoeuvred us either 'full astern or full ahead.' We were darting all over the place with this 20-knot ship, which was almost acrobatic in its exercise.'

Tom brightens up:

'Anyway, we made it to Malta and we were given some special berth under a cliff in Marsaslokk Bay, supposedly out of sight. We then off-loaded the ammunition and petrol that these people needed so desperately. I must be honest, I did keep a couple of tins of petrol for my own personal use. We stayed in Malta for quite a while, it was pretty safe.'

It was not for long though, as there was work to be done. Tom explains:

'We then went to Alexandria to load up with similar cargo to bring back to Malta. It became quite tedious, one trip after another, thirteen forays in all. It was a good year. The Italians were after us the whole time! The Italian battleship, *Vittoria*, made us her special target but she just couldn't get the measure of us, as we did not suffer a single hit!'

Tom's sense of pride shows through in the tone of his voice. There were some exceptional times during the war and the connections made during and after became quite personal, independent of the side that one fought on.

A connection for Tom, which he recalls very fondly:

'The Gunnery Officer in *Vittoria* was a charming chap, Count Tuleio Angheben. I met him after the war, when he was in command of a little liner. He became a great friend of mine when I was in Malta in the 50's, during my time in NATO. I remember how *Vittoria* tried so hard to get us, she came out two or three times, all hands on deck, we used to say a prayer, we were very very sincere! I remarked to Tuleio the first time we met after the war: "You missed. A lot of failed attempts!'

Tom underplays and understates how difficult and trying those times must have been with a special statement:

'We had many interesting journeys.'

I think that is a rather delightful way of talking about these forays from Alexandria to Malta and back again. There were many Italian Cant dive bombers about, which Tom rated highly:

'They were made with Bristol engines, had wooden bodies and so burned pretty quickly. Once when we were on passage from Malta to Alexandria we were entertained by them for lunch. George Graham and I were given ample time to get our personal Pom-pom going! We heard the usual, pom-pom noise, nothing happened much, but again, pom-pom, then a Cant came too close and caught it. I stood and watched it burn. It delighted our crew members. I was on the bridge when this happened. For those of you who don't know, 'pom-pom' was slang for the Bofors Anti-Aircraft gun, which made a 'Pom Pom' noise when it was firing.

'I had become pretty chummy with the Captain and asked him if we could pick up any survivors. I was told negative, this got back to the Commander, who said we would get in a lot of trouble if we didn't pick up these survivors. The Captain was not happy with this but told us to call a destroyer up and thought that that would be the end of it.

'Among the survivors was the pilot, whom I later knew in NATO. He got on well in the Italian Air Force after the war. Funnily enough, he was appointed to NATO in Malta at the time that I was there, and we became real friends. He used to help me out with the Fiat distributor in Malta. He had a lovely wife as well. The saying, It's a small world seemed to win true even more so then than nowadays.'

Not all voyages between the two ports were fun though:

'One of the thirteen trips between Malta and Alexandria was to clear out remaining fifth columnists and 'ne-er-do-wells.' We were asked to take them out of Malta via Alexandria, where they would eventually get to Kenya to fend for themselves for the rest of the war. This trip involved a very important notoriety.

'The Chief Justice, Sir Arturo Mercecha, his wife, and daughter, Lilian, were brought on board. I was close to the Captain by then, suggesting a nice suite for the Chief Justice on our ship. I told the Captain this chap was off to Kenya and deserved a good trip before then. The Captain was not impressed. I had to give him the same accommodation as the rest. However, I did not let it lie there. I leaked the news to the Governor's ADC, asking him to sort it out. I was very calculating really: I knew the Captain and Governor were to have lunch together and, as planned, the Governor asked where the Chief Justice was being housed. He also suggested that he must be given a suite, especially as there was one available. Happily, he got the suite.'

It was another of those events and kind actions that Tom took during the war that followed him around afterwards. He mentions:

'When I went back to Malta in NATO, Sir Arturo Mercecha was just retiring, and Lilian had married the Ford's distributor on the Island, a chap called Joe Gasan. Anyway, she was having a big party, as they were high up in Maltese circles. I had just arrived on the island, so we attended; Lilian remembered me and wished my wife and myself a really happy tour with NATO. She helped us during our stay there quite a bit.'

Tom hesitates, he has remembered a sad event, going back to a previous ship:

'There was a final sad exploit with *HMS Breconshire*. I had sold the new Imperial motorbike to the police force and bought a Rudge Whitworth in Alexandria and decided to keep it there, as things were getting a bit difficult in Malta. Sadly, on one occasion the *Queen Elizabeth* was mined in Alexandria, it was the Autumn of 1941. A friend of George Graham's and I had gone to a dance hall, moaning to each other that these beautiful Lebanese girls would never become detached from their mothers, who followed them everywhere. I forgot which side of the road I should have been driving on. Well, the events moved quite fast after that - an Arab bus that was making towards us went through a shop window. Well, we did not wait to see the result which, I heard later, was a few minor scratches. However, we wasted no time in getting back on board *Breconshire*. Golly, I was pretty scared now, I crept back on board and placed the bike back in its allotted spot and awaited developments. It wasn't long before the Naval Police came aboard to see if any of the officers had been out that evening, in Alexandria. My chum George Graham was the

Officer-in-Charge for the day and so he could satisfy the police that we hadn't let any of our officers, go ashore!

'We also noticed that the Naval Patrol was showing a huge interest in the *Queen Elizabeth*, berthed near to us, having received warning that she was going to be torpedoed. We were often receiving false alarms and as it was past midnight, we turned in. A few hours later there was absolute chaos. As I said, we were berthed close by, so we perhaps had a better view of the proceedings.

'A cadet from the *Queen Elizabeth* came along to our ship saying our Electrical Officer was required to report on board. Well, we were able to piece the events together afterwards. Two Italian Navy Officers had appeared on the quay and quietly walked up the *Queen Elizabeth's* gangway, saluted the Officer-of-the-Watch and requested to speak to the Duty Commanding Officer, all this carried out in perfect English. They had secured a mine of some kind to the ship's side, about midships. How they were able to do it is a mystery. They had come from an Italian submarine, now well out of the way. By now the Commander had arrived and more saluting went on. The immediate idea was to lock the Italian Officers up in the compartment nearest to the mine, hoping this might assist them to show how it could be diffused. The Italians agreed, but regretted that there was no safety device built into it. All the local brains then examined the mine, without touching it, and they agreed with the Italians. The Italians gave the time when the mine would explode and implored the Captain to evacuate the ship. This he refused to do, but he ordered all personnel below the Upper Deck to come aloft. The Italians then gave away some more information, which resulted in fewer casualties. However, the mine went off in the early morning causing considerable damage.

'There are many incidents where Italians have performed individually, or in small numbers, some brave feats. I am already reminded of Tuleio Angheben, which I will tell you about later, taking his little liner, the *Citta de Benghazi*, out of Malta's harbour with a huge mine attached to the anchor. Such a great feat saved the Grand Harbour at Malta from a large explosion.'

Quietly, Tom continues:

'Anyway, I returned the motorbike to the shop, the next day, when things had settled down. I knew we weren't going to have an easy trip on *HMS Breconshire* so I had decided to leave it with the shop owner, saying it may be some time before I would be coming back. We had the *Clan Chathen* with us, doing exercises together. We received news that the Italian fleet had every available spare ship coming along to intercept us. The Germans and Italians both had a squadron of bombers standing by and the great battleship, *Vittoria*, was also there. We managed to avoid all of them, surviving a night of torpedoes criss-crossing through the water. We saw Malta ahead, couldn't believe it, we were not far from the island, only two or three miles off. Our Gunnery Officer was tired, we all were. I was on the bridge, a signal came through to say that some Spitfires had arrived in Malta and would be scrambled to our assistance within the next hour. Naturally, we watched for them.

'Messerschmidt 109s (Me 109s) don't look unlike Spitfires in the sky at night. We were told to let them pass, we did, but they were Me 109s! Unfortunately, one did very well with its bomb, which exploded underneath our ship. It didn't do a lot of damage but cracked the injector valves from the big diesel engines and they both stopped. The very brilliant Lt-Comd Kennedy, our Second Engineer, could not get the engines going, manna from heaven for the Italians and Germans.

However, the Spitfires arrived and protected us for the rest of that day. The Cruisers, *HMS Aurora* and *HMS Penelope* tried to tow us, but the effort just ripped their capstans out of the deck.

'We resorted to a second plan: two paddle tugs from Malta came out when it was dark, the *Robust* and *Ancient*, and took us in tow, manned by Officers from the cruisers, bringing us to safety, yet again, in the bay at Halfar, near to the Naval Air Station. We anchored there and awaited developments for the next day.

'The other side were not slow in finding us as we were not in good shelter, only being able to get to the middle of this lovely harbour. We soon ran out of ammunition. The Royal Malta Artillery did the very best that they could and brought a lot of the bombers down. My friend, the RMA Officer Commanding, and later Fiat Distributor, Major Henny Scicluna, was an absolute ace at helping people in trouble with his relentless artillery barrage. The other side, however, about five o'clock that day, using Junkers 87s, set up an assault on us and although we managed to shoot down a couple of them, one of them gave us a direct hit.

'The bomb went down our Number 3 hatch and exploded amongst the coal. It was policy then to have cargo, such as coal, at the top, with petrol stored below, just for that reason. Auxiliary engines were responsible for making sure that there was pressure in the hoses, but as these engines were not working we couldn't get water to the fire in the hatch.'

Tom hesitates, taking stock:

'It got very bad. It would have been worse if it had got to the petrol but then we found another bomb had exploded underneath the ship and we were leaking. The ship was very quietly sinking and the Captain ordered 'Abandon Ship.' A little Maltese drifter came alongside and we just quietly got into it. The ship was getting a battering by then and soon after we had left, it turned over.

'It was very sad, we had left some pedal cycles in the Number 1 hatch. Six of them George and I had bought for friends in Malta. Reluctantly, and without much intention, we said that the next day we would try and get some of the cargo out, but it didn't help very much, the ship was too unstable. It was salvaged after the war. We did manage to get out the fuel and some of the ammunition, so we were able to sail in *HMS Penelope* and *HMS Aurora* to Gibraltar.'

At this point, Tom makes a lovely, poignant statement:

'The Captain of *HMS Breconshire* was a brilliant man, that is why that ship survived for so long.'

To have been through so much and still think about other people's attributes is one of Tom's great characteristics. However at the time, he had other things to think about, too!

'George Graham and I both went sick. I caught pneumonia. We went to the Naval Hospital at Bighi. However, we were told that we would have to be evacuated from Malta in a hospital ship. It never came. We healed, and then planned for the great Ohio convoy.

'Our Captain was the Chief Staff Officer for the operation at the time. All C-in-C staff, many having had two years on *HMS Breconshire*, proved they were well-experienced, and were called up for this next operation also. It showed how the Admiralty was short of officers and, in any case, could not get them to Malta at the time. Graham, myself and a few others, who were required in the UK for other duties, were allocated to aircraft which flew us from Malta to Cairo, then by onward transport by sea to the UK. I was rather sad as I had had a good time with the *HMS Breconshire*, whose Captain was Cecil Alexander Gordon Hutcheson, RN.

'The aircraft we were in, an RAF Lockheed Lodestar, touched down, refuelled and then went to the end of the airstrip and took off again. The other side gave us hell. It was an incredibly difficult operation as we were not allowed to use any lights for any part of the landing and take off, but we were airborne and away. There was a choice of Cairo or Alexandria as to where to stay. Naturally, I wished to get my motorbike back from Alexandria, and that is what I attempted to do! I then received just the worst news of all: the chap had flogged it! Luck was in for me, though; there was the battle cruiser there, *HMS Repulse*. A connection of mine, a Bristolian, the Dental Officer on board the depot ship, Anthony Wells, was a real charmer. Anyway, he rang a few mates, of whom Baker Pasha was one. This friend was the Police Chief, a Bristolian also. What a stroke of luck! He found out where it had gone and got it back by lunchtime the very next day. He, Baker Pasha, went straight to the shop and, reprimanding the chap, found the bike at the back of the shop where he had it hidden.'

Tom stayed a while in Alexandria waiting for transport to the UK and one particular evening, still using this bike went out to dinner with the Royal Gloucestershire Hussars somewhere in the desert. 'Well, we got stuck in the sand with this bike and it took several soldiers to lift it for about half a mile before we managed to get it on its way. That bike was always in one scrap or another.'

There was always one event or another which kept things in perspective at all times. From there, Tom traces the final trip home.

'We went to Suez to join the great troop ship, the *New Amsterdam*, which took us to Cape Town. From there we went on board the *Windsor Castle*, onward to the UK. These ships were very modern and safe, we didn't have one emergency at any stage of that trip home and arrived back in Liverpool about

May of 1942. I got home to Bristol without much problem and was overjoyed to find that the chap at the Bewdley garage had rebuilt my MG. The money I had saved up from my time on *HMS Breconshire* paid for it.

'I had bought a Rudge in Alexandria for £35 and sold it later for £28. However, I had more than £7 worth of fun out of it.'

*

Chapter 4
on HMS Bulolo,
Algiers, Sicily, Anzio
May 1942 to June 1944

So Tom returned to Liverpool on board the Union Castle ship, *SS Windsor Castle*. He bought oranges for his family en route and went over to Bewdley to pick up the £35 MG, as he had been given two weeks leave before going back to *HMS Mersey* to reconstruct the accounts of *HMS Breconshire*.

Tom continues:

'Most of the accounts were okay, but some had to be extended to make them more formal. The Commodore, Richard Percival Gayler, RNR, who had been on the Clan Line all his life, was extremely good to the young officers. I liked him a lot.'

While doing this reconstruction work, Tom was given an appointment in *HMS Bulolo*, but he couldn't join for some months. This was no hardship to Tom:

'There was lots of work, we always had a system for it and at the same time it was great fun in the *Mersey*. I must be honest, after that, we all drifted apart, and so it went on. The work that we were doing was being carried out in the old David Lewis Northern Hospital. While I was still there I had a rather unfortunate time with a WREN and my MG. I was supposed to have the WREN back by 10.30 that evening but was a bit tight on timing, so I put my foot down. Well, the crankshaft broke! There were bits everywhere. I had to get the girl to help me; she and I pushed it back and I managed to find a garage to put it in, and that was the end of that pleasant evening together. The next day, I phoned my brother-in-law at

Bewdley, whom I asked to come up and tow me back to his home. I thought that I could then take the crankshaft out of the other car that I had there, but actually I found a new one for £10 a little later on. The real fun was taking the car back to Bewdley! My brother-in-law had a fast Opel, everyone hated it but it did go; I have never been so frightened in all my life as I was in that car that night! The roads between Liverpool and Bewdley are not good and I was really surprised that it ever got there at all. Frightened me to death. The car was repaired in due course. I had to stay in as I couldn't afford to go out and then I received this draft to say that I would join *HMS Bulolo* on the following Tuesday, on the ship's return from the Algiers landing!'

Tom was very excited about this prospect because there was so much secrecy concerning this ship:

'*Bulolo* seemed to be a very Special Service ship; whenever there was any landing to speak about, she was there. She was a Combined Operations Headquarters ship which took the Admiral, the General, the Air Marshall and their staff into all the landings, until it was safe for them to move to their HQs ashore.'

On the assigned day, Tom remembers his welcome:

'Everything on board looked very clean and pristine. I was a lieutenant by then and I was met with: "Your relief is waiting to welcome you." Actually, we had known each other before, we had been junior pursers together with the P & O. He was a chap called Butcher. We had a drink or two and reminisced.'

By then, there were only two or three days until Butcher left and Tom took over his job as the Captain's Secretary. Butcher had been the secretary since the start of the war. This particular captain was the oldest sea-going captain in the Royal Navy. Tom recalls how he loved sunbathing without any clothes on: 'A Chief Petty Officer was asked if there was anything in sight and he replied, very dryly, "No, only the old man!"' Tom chuckles at this.

The first landing in which *Bulolo* had been involved was Operation Torch, in North Africa, in November 1942, when she went into Algiers. Although Tom spent time aboard *Bulolo* on a number of exercises before being posted to the ship, he did not join it until 9 February 1943, so he was not present at Operation Torch. However, he knew a number of people who were, who told him what went on:

'*HMS Bulolo* was the HQ ship for the first important landing, in Algiers. We had every confidence that we would not have a lot of trouble in getting the French to come over to our side. It was late 1942 by then. The French had enough fire-power on their ships, and guns on headlands, to blow us out of the water, but we were pretty sure that our intelligence people had done a good job of sorting this out.

'The day before the landing the German air force were showing us that they really did not like us being there. We had some Sea Fires as well as Anti-Aircraft Guns, but their Ju 88's were stronger and they started to drop bombs on us. One of these, a few cables off our starboard side, deluged us with water, but nothing more than that.

'We met up with the French Admiral, Darlan, who did not like us because of the mess we had made of his battleship *Jules Verne*, so we were unsure how he would react to us now. Well, Admiral Burroughs wanted to make sure that we made a spectacular entrance and told Captain Hamer of his intentions. We had all the right charts and we knew which side of the pier we needed to get to. So off we went, and at some fantastic speed as well! The Engineer Commander, Bill Monteith, Royal Australian Navy Reserve, one of the world's great characters who excelled himself at every landing, watched the progress of *Bulolo* from the office window. Well, Bill got up to the trick of talking to the Engineer Officer on the telephone in the engine room and asked him if he had received any movements from the bridge. If the Captain knew that it was the Engineer Officer who was commanding the ship, he would not have been best pleased! Well, Bill told the chap to go slow ahead and slow right down, we were going too fast. The Chief Engineer commanded Emergency Full Astern from the engine room; vital seconds were wasted, the Chief had given the order too late and they went straight into the piles at the end of the pier. We did some damage to the bows but we didn't hurt anyone. We stopped okay and made a spectacular entrance! It was a good job Bill had already alerted the Engine Room.

'Well, Admiral Burroughs and the French Commander got together and we did all join up. It could have been a disaster but it wasn't due to Bill's actions. We learned later that the reason why no orders of movements given from the bridge to the engine room had been received was due to a bomb splinter, which had stuck in the oil pipe which activated the engine telegraph. The telegraph should have been checked before entering harbour, but with all the excitement it was not done. The whole incident wanted a bit of sorting out but no disciplinary charges were brought. Some of the French thought we had done it purposely, to make a spectacular entrance!'

Tom remembers that there were certain aspects of *Bulolo* that were understood on both sides:

'*Bulolo* received very special attention from the Germans. Not surprisingly, for it transpired later that all German warship captains carried a silhouette of *Bulolo* as a prime target. But they still never managed to knock her out!'

Tom continues: 'We undertook various exercises but we didn't move until the early part of 1943, when a huge convoy was assembled. Joining it, we went around to Port Tewfiq, at the southern end of the Suez Canal.

'All sorts of people turned up to see us off. Winston Churchill came to wish us well, it was all absolutely fantastic! Everybodys' phone calls were recorded, tape recorders were 'two a penny', they were not even thought of on shore! Of course, we had to keep quiet about that, but it was wonderful. Everybody seemed to be hand-picked for the ship and the captain was more easy-going than the captain of the *Breconshire*.

'Admiral Lord Louis Mountbatten came and went quite often. The ship was his idea, and he insisted it had to be at the very high standard of efficiency that it was. Well, the convoy got going and we went off to Cape Town and then Durban.

'We had a young South African Lieutenant, Robert Ellis-Brown from Durban aboard who was in the South African Navy Volunteer Reserve. His father, the Mayor of Durban, owned a department store, so when we arrived there we had a big bash; lovely food, which we had missed, and lots of girls came to the party. We had the pick of the bunch of these girls in Durban and they were very different! Actually, of the girls we met in Durban, two of them subsequently married their respective companions, both officers. I and a friend were at battle stations vying for one girl; however, neither of us got very far. Mr Ellis-Brown, the Mayor, did us well at that party. Gave us this super banquet in the Town Hall and we had a lovely forty-eight hours.

'I thought my first landing was going to be at Rangoon, but fortunately that was cancelled. Instead, the landing was in Sicily, Operation Husky. It was superbly organised. We did one exercise and then another and by the time July 1943 arrived we had everything absolutely spot on. The Italians didn't realise that we were coming at all; they thought we were doing the same old trip to Malta again. When we got to Malta there were plenty of supplies, food, fuel and fun, and then we were off to Sicily. I don't know how or why, but they found it strange that we had arrived! We lay off Syracuse for a total of three weeks.

'Our radar was manned by Wing Commander "Sally" Sarell; it was a very secret radar, housed in a hut. I saw my first plane shot down at night from the workings of that radar system. Anyway, "Sally" invited me along to the hut. He had two Beaufighters (the pride of Bristol) flying around and he was talking to these two planes when they spotted a Ju88. After a while there was a resounding flash - and one Ju88 no longer existed! Naturally, the whole thing was done with the greatest subterfuge and we had to keep our great superiority in this area a secret, especially shooting down enemy aircraft at night.'

Tom explains further about this great ship that he was in:

'Actually *HMS Bulolo* was an Australian Merchant liner, built for Burns, Philip & Co Ltd for the Australia-to-New Guinea service. At the outbreak of the war she was converted to an Armed Merchant Cruiser based at Cape Town, hence we had a resounding welcome when we got there. She had been refitted in UK for her new role of Combined Operations Headquarters Ship. Another HQ Ship was the *Largs*, an old French fruit ship formerly called *Charles Plumier*. She was much smaller, and not so liberally fitted out, but was still very useful.'

Another benefit of being in *HMS Bulolo* becomes apparent:

'When we left the Clyde in the big convoy going to Suez we were one of the first RN Ships to carry WRENs! Well, imagine my excitement when the Flag Captain told me that we were going to have eighty WRENs on board! They arrived in a drifter, with a not so lovely but very capable lady in charge of them. She was a jolly good disciplinarian. We made part of the mess deck into a cinema with fifty seats and we used to show them a film sometimes to entertain them. An old favourite was James Cagney in 'Yankee Doodle Dandy' but alas, there was no-one as interesting or attractive out of this group of eighty as the girlfriend that I had just said goodbye to in the UK. Not so, however, for my chums, most of whom had their own little WREN.'

Tom, apparently, did find a little mischief aboard though: 'We went on with these lovely young WRENs aboard, one thing led to another and I rather let myself go with one of them, engaging in pleasantries one evening. Well, the door of the captain's cabin under the bridge opened and the Captain came out on deck! Fortunately, it was a very dark night. He fell over us where we were sitting and there were lots of oaths and dreadful language and then he disappeared very quickly up the ladder to the bridge. I rushed back to the Captain's office. The phone rang immediately and the Captain said: 'Tom, you will never believe what has just happened. I fell over someone carrying on with one of those damn WRENs. Get the Commander up on the bridge right now!'

'I never told the Commander it was me the Captain was telling him about. When he asked me what we should do about the situation I told him about the barbed wire we were carrying in the Number 3 hold and suggested that it might be used in some way to solve the problem. The wretched barbed wire was brought out and placed all around the WRENs accommodation. It was rather a waste of time really, since people continued with their naughty practices. The WRENs disappeared when we got to the Suez and that was that.'

Tom seemed disappointed that they had gone but soon turned his attention to the Suez:

'Well, we finished the landing at Syracuse, all was well, at last the Allies had landed and we were then going on to Bombay, which, of course, was in a very, very sad situation.

But there was not much risk of subs in the Indian Ocean and off we sailed through the Red Sea to the Indian Ocean.

'A rather terrible thing happened one afternoon. Lieutenant Graham Barton-Hilton and myself were on the Emergency Bridge, sunbathing with no clothes on. There was lots of mud around the ship, we felt this nasty jerk, all seemed to be okay, it had only been momentary, and the ship steamed on as usual. But I rushed down to the office immediately and the phone rang. It was the Captain, who was very concerned. He ordered me to bring the King's Regulations and Admiralty Instructions and we looked through them thoroughly. He told me that there did not seem to be any damage and he did not wish to enter the incident in the log. I was a good Secretary to the Captain; I said he should enter it in the log as a 'soft landing.' He, however, decided that he wouldn't put it in at all. Well, it got a bit messy. I called the officer who was on the Bridge at the time, and he agreed with the Captain. Then I called in the Navigating Officer, Lt-Cdr Robert Mayo, who did not like the situation one bit and took my side, suggesting it should be logged. Well, Mayo then backed off a bit and suggested that maybe he should have noticed that the Officer on Watch was ten miles off course! So that was that. It was not logged and I had to tell the Commander that that would be the end of it. It was a very tricky situation.'

'Well, we arrived in Bombay. It was a really splendid occasion. Admiral Lord Louis Mountbatten, Commander in Chief and in charge of Combined Operations, was there. He made a great speech, saying that for the next landing there should be real secrecy, nobody should know about it. Well, he knew that we had all been working pretty flat-out for six months and suggested that the crew really needed a week's leave. The Lower Deck went raving mad, there would be good talent around, lots of girls, and they would be 'Harry Flakers' every night.

'Graham Barton-Hilton and I went off to one of the hill stations near Bombay - took the mainline train and then changed to a little hill railway that went up the side of the mountain. We arrived at a place called Matheran where there were no ladies around, just lots of old people. We played some tennis and spent a lot of time walking the countryside. We stayed four days, just generally enjoying a relaxing time, but on the fourth day we found a note telling us get the train back to Bombay pretty sharpish as we were required to get back to *Bulolo*. The Captain, Captain Richard Hamer RN, was being court-martialled because he had run aground and not reported it properly!

'Graham and I returned immediately. At the time, our ship was in dry dock and, of course, they found a dent in the hull while it was there. It was reported to Lord Louis himself, who was furious that it had not been reported, and so the Captain was court-martialled.'

Tom remembers a huge coincidence of his time in *Bulolo*, whilst they were in Bombay. He came across a chap called Brown, with whom he had been at Wellington. Brown was now the Admiral's Secretary, Royal Indian Navy, and they had met several years earlier there when Tom was in *Strathnaver*. Brown was going to play a part in the court-martial:

'I asked him if he could find someone to stand up for my captain. I was told to keep out of it, but Brown did find a chap, a Barrister, who put in a very big plea for him as the oldest sea-going captain - going on 70. But he was inevitably found guilty of stranding his ship, was dismissed his command immediately and ordered back to the UK to become the Naval Officer in Charge at Thurso, Scotland, where he remained until the end of the war. It was such a shame, he was a real legend, a tough chap. He and I had a little dinner in his cabin the night before he left. I thought I would be going with him, but it was not to be. The Commander took on the temporary command of the ship and the very next day I started clearing up my belongings thinking that the new Captain, whoever he would be, would be bringing his own Secretary with him.

'There was a knock on my cabin door and I was told that Captain Kershaw would like to see me. It appeared that they had already found a new captain for the ship. I entered his cabin, the room was all redone and he looked as if he meant business. In a big gruff voice he told me to sit down.

'Kershaw said that he didn't suffer fools gladly and that he had a way of getting rid of unwanted people. He told me that he had an Indian as his Secretary but that the chap suffered from seasickness, so he would take me on instead. He said that I would have to work and work like hell, and in return he would give me a good and fair report and I would get on in my career. He asked if I thought I was up to it? Of course, I said that I would be honoured to be his Secretary. He was as good as his word. In fact, he was fantastic! Instead of being a run-of-the-mill ship it became the byword of the whole Fleet. The ship was notoriously smart, absolutely super, right through the war. Everything we did was done by the book.

'Kershaw lasted about two-and-a-half years with the ship and was then promoted, but I couldn't go with him as it was decided that the Secretary should stay with the ship to keep some continuity in its running.'

Tom tells us of the general running of the ship, at this point: 'There were a constant stream of Officers leaving the ship, you have got to have a good reason to get rid of people, but as Captain Kershaw had been a Chief of Staff to Lord Mountbatten it didn't seem to be a problem. We had a very, very efficient team of officers. As the days ticked by we realised that we were being groomed. As we carried out two or three interesting exercises along the coast south of Bombay, rumours started up about a landing to have a go at Rangoon. However, the landing was called off as the losses would have been unacceptable due to the Japanese holding the River Irriwaddy. The whole thing packed up and the force we were with was sent back to Port Tewfiq.

'Then we started exercises again, the target, of course, being Sicily. We achieved an impeccably high standard moving through the Suez Canal back to Malta. We stayed in Grand Harbour for a couple of days. Malta itself was near enough back to peacetime life. There was plenty of everything and they really did deserve it, as they had been through so much bombing in 1942.

'From Sicily we moved on to Naples, which had only recently fallen to Allied hands. There was such a mess in the bay, with sunken ships in the harbour. Our guys and the Americans soon put it all right and we settled down in Naples because we knew that we were going to have a go in two weeks or so at Anzio: Operation Shingle.

'There was much secrecy kept about this landing. The meetings I went to with the Captain told me this anyway. It did take a while for the information to come out. Nobody seemed worried about this target. However, we were very, very wrong! Eventually the time came to embark for the landing, which wasn't far from the Naples base. Our aim was to encircle a whole lot of Germans, so we arrived in pitch black on 21st January 1944, proceeded ashore and were greeted with all hell. Shells and bombs fell everywhere. Very fortunately, with the various devices we had on *Bulolo*, we didn't get hit. The Hospital ship near us was sunk and we had to take on board the staff, there being no patients as yet, luckily. It was a wicked thing to do, there had been red crosses everywhere on the ship and she was well lit up, but one of the German aircraft bombed her. There were lots of casualties as well.

'We went on as we had to, as *Bulolo* was the HQ at sea, and with all this tremendous opposition it was taking a lot longer for us to get the chaps ashore, the Flag Officer, General and Air Marshall, that is. We were glad to get out and back to Naples. We were too near the front line for comfort and felt little amusement at all the goings on.

'Admiral Tom Troubridge was our Admiral for the landings for *Bulolo*. He was very approachable, so at ease. I remember at Anzio how he pointed out a six-foot square on the bridge saying he wanted that bit to himself when we were under attack. He would often check out the food that the crew were having as well, good and bad, just to make sure every- thing was okay for the chaps. Anyway, from Naples we went to Algiers to lay up for a few weeks.

'Admiral Troubridge did not go with us, sadly; he went to a small Headquarters ship which had just been converted called *The Royal Ulsterman*. We had received news of the prepara- tions for the Second Front being planned at home, and apparently Troubridge would be needed for part of this, based in Southern France. We rowed him across to the other ship according to the very best traditions, but before he went he sent for me and said he knew all about the little MG back at home! He showed me a cask full of red wine which he had managed to acquire in Naples and inferred that he needed to get it home; told me that he wanted me to put it in my MG and take it around to his wife when we got to the UK! I asked him what I was to do about the Customs and he rattled off the name of the Customs Officer who was a chum of his, telling me that I wouldn't have any problems there.

'*Bulolo* stayed in Algiers for a while, we had a lovely time but we were pleased to learn that we were going back to the Clyde. We all felt concerned that our luck may not last!

'There we were, wonderful weather through the Bay of Biscay, it was early February, early Spring really, we even did some sunbathing right up to the level of Bordeaux, but then it turned to good old typical English weather, cooler and wet.'

From the Clyde, *Bulolo* sailed to Portland and Tom remembered his mission with the cask of Admiral's wine:

'I did not have a car at Portland so I waited till we were at Southampton and made sure that my car was still fairly reliable. Captain Kershaw gave me a morning off to get rid of the cask, so I stuck it in the back of the MG and off I went. I really wondered what was going to happen at the dock gate. The barrel had Admiral Troubridge's name on it and when the Customs Officer was called out and took a look at my goods in the back of the car he just told me to get on with it. So off I went. I found his house, a couple of miles north of Southampton. His wife offered me coffee and then lunch, which I stayed for, and then I headed back to the ship. I had a letter from the Admiral, later on: thought it was super of him to take time out to thank me.

'Things changed on *Bulolo* after that. Straight away at Portland various people from Admiralty, Bath arrived on board with instruments. It was obvious that we were going to have a bit of a refit so that she was right up to date with all the new bits and pieces for surveillance and communication. A refit conference was held and it was decided that lots of the jobs would take a good month: we all reckoned we could settle down for a month, at least. I went home and got the MG going and put it in a disused warehouse alongside the ship. I also found a phone there, in the warehouse, that was working. I told Graham Barton-Hilton and the Supply Officer, Mike Hutton, another P & O Officer who wished me to return to that organisation after the war, and so we were able to speak to our nearest and dearest as often as we wished. We were very careful, and nobody ever found out about the phone. No-one seemed worried that we were using this warehouse. A troop ship came by with lots of Americans who stayed in the warehouse and watched our work. Lots of them were very taken by the style of the MG and I took a Lieutenant-Colonel out in mine for a spin: he was most impressed.

'Meanwhile, I was very busy with all the orders coming through, all very secret. I brought the reports up to date and then showed them to Captain Kershaw, who told me that there was to be a secret meeting near to Petersfield and that I would go with him. Churchill, Eisenhower, General Smutts and others were all there. Smutts was a great chap, very old, but he gave us some jolly good questions to answer. The best part of all of this secrecy was that the Germans had no idea of the actual date of whatever they thought we were up to! 5th June, it was, and then it was postponed to 6th June. I knew this date way before, but I couldn't tell anyone at all. I kept this to myself and I thought it was a huge responsibility for me, a chap in his early 20's.

'There was a new Admiral then, Admiral Douglas-Pennant, and also Admiral Robertshaw (he was my Admiral later, when I was in NATO). I said once to Teddy Astley-Jones (Robertshaw's Secretary) that I had to nick petrol all the time to take Kershaw everywhere. Well, jolly good job that I did tell him. Teddy told me to come back the next morning for my G Licence. Admiral Robertshaw was so helpful, oh yes, said it was for Kershaw's Secretary, so he signed for it and really it was all so simple. All I had to do was to sign a form at the garage that I went to, show this G licence and I got all the petrol that I wanted. Fuel became no problem for me at all.'

Taking a break from the rigours of duty, Tom always has a story to tell about Kershaw: 'We did have our ups and downs. On one occasion, we were all ready to go to our homes for the weekend, Captain Kershaw was entertaining a lady friend and I thought that as soon as he was ready, I could go. Well, my leading Writer, Reginald Holmes, a big shirt manufacturer from Ashton-under-Lyne, told me that if I couldn't drive the captain, he could. So that helped me a great deal but on this occasion I was not able to go. One week or so before, an officer in the Royal Marines said he knew that I took out drink and cigarettes in my car. He asked me if it was easy but I said I didn't want to say or offer any kind of advice on the subject. He said that I seemed to get away with it all right. Anyway I forgot about this until the Saturday of the leave weekend, when I was just waiting to get the 'all clear' to go. The Customs Officer phoned me and said he had a Marine officer with him who was being detained for having some gin and cigarettes! He couldn't let it go because the Customs Officer had too many subordinates watching, so he had to make an example. So I had to stay on and write a report. Worse still, it broke up the Captain's luncheon party. I had to phone the Admiral's Secretary and say that the Captain would like to see the Admiral straight away. This was the Port Admiral, Southampton. Reluctantly, the Secretary said that we could go over then and there. The Admiral wasn't pleased to see us and suggested that I write the circumstantial letter for court-martial. As the conversation continued Captain Kershaw managed to get some sense into the Admiral; put it to him that we were all sailors and swinging the lamp a bit was no big problem. The Admiral agreed and suggested that the Captain officially admonish the officer and put it in the log. By 3.00 p.m. we all managed to go on our way. The officer didn't do it again!

'The refit was ready, the ship was bristling with communications and close-quarters AA armament, everything was there. *Bulolo* was a highly sophisticated communications craft capable of simultaneously transmitting and receiving on 146 frequencies. She was armed with various weapons; 6 inch guns (7 in total), 3 inch Anti-Aircraft guns (2 of these) and several close-range weapons. We quietly sailed up to Portsmouth with lots of Dockyard maties on board. I, very naughtily, took my girlfriend along! No-one saw her, no-one knew. Well not up until now! We did two or three exercises which were very important and we all learnt even more. We had landing craft on both sides of our boat decks. They had even thought of all sorts of patents to make it easier to lower them if it was blowing hard. They had adapted the landing craft gear to take all these new ideas and we were really at the greatest pitch of efficiency that we could be at, on what was already an efficient ship.'

*

Tom at Wellington School, Somerset with
Boris, the family pet, 1930.

Admiral Burroughs, Algiers 1942.

The French Admiral, Admiral Darlan boarding *HMS Bulolo*, Algiers 1942.

Admiral Somerville with Captain Hamer, Algiers 1942.

Luftwaffe aircraft crew captured in Algiers, 1942.

Major Roosevelt, (on left) President Roosevelt's son, talking to a Journalist on board *HMS Bulolo*, Algiers 1942.

En route to the Casablanca Conference, 1943.

Mr Winston Churchill addressing *Bulolo's* ship's Company in Casablanca, 1943.

HM King George VI with Captain (later Admiral) B. Robertshaw D.S.O., Chief Staff
Officer during Operation Overlord, Normandy 1944.

Part of Main Signals Office, *HMS Bulolo* 1944.

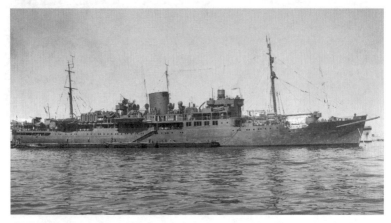

HMS Bulolo, Headquarters Ship for Admirals Ramsey and Douglas-Pennant and Generals Dempsey and Graham directing JUNO Sector Landing, Operation Overlord, Normandy, June 1944.

Commander E. B. Clark
(Second-in-Command) R.N.

Captain C. A. Kershaw R.N.
(in Command)

Eng' Lt. Com' W. Monteith
R.A.N.R. (S)
(Chief Engineer)

Pay' Lieut T. H. Foden
R.N.R
(Captains Sec')

Lieut Com' R.N. Mayo R.N.R.
(Navigator)

Five Invasion N.O.s : by Commander Tom S. Lee, R.N.

Here are some of the officers of one of H.M. ships which took a big part in the successful combined operations in Normandy. Capt. Kershaw is well remembered as the Navy and England Rugger player and fencer. He is also, as has been recently proved, a very good team selector

A cartoon of Tom and four of the Invasion Naval Officers, 1944.

Admiral Lord Louis Mountbatten taking the Japanese surrender, Singapore 1945.

Chapter 5
On HMS Bulolo, Normandy
June 1944 to December 1946

'We went into the Solent and got rid of all the iron-mongery into a garage in Southampton. The weather was ghastly, we were told that we would be getting ready on the night of 4th to land on 5th but Eisenhower postponed it to the 6th due to the bad weather. The Germans thought that we would land in the Calais area, so they were not expecting us to land where we did.

'We got in close to the shore at Juno Beach, on the morning of the 6th. The air activity was superb, ours and theirs, they were using the new radial-engined fighter, the Focke Wulf 190. One came through at us and let her bombs go. These were phosphorous bombs, they both hit us and I lost three of my really good chums. Two of these chums were Flight Lieutenants who were on the night-fighter equipment. They had done their stuff in keeping the enemy aircraft away from us in all the other landings. They were off-watch in their bunks, as were two young RNVR's who worked as cipher officers as well. Very sad.

'We were told that if anything happened to us all resources must be directed into keeping the ship going. If the *Bulolo* was out of action for more than two minutes, the Admiral said, the whole landing would have to be called off. Well, even though these bombs had hit us and we were all terribly worried as the German opposition was fantastic, we kept on going.

'Our Chief Engineer, Bill Monteith really was brilliant. The decorations that he received were justly deserved. At every landing he was the star of the scene. By the end of the war he had a DSC and bar. On this occasion he led the Damage Control Team with great efficiency and they put the fire out very, very quickly. The ship was back under control; the electrics had gone off but they got them going in a minute. The ship lost very little time and all was well except for the officer's Accommodation Mess, where the bombs had hit. The fighter who bombed us was then shot down but the pilot survived and was brought back on board for us to interrogate. This was necessary, as we still had all the important chaps on board. They had not gone ashore by then. This young German stayed for a day on board, then went to the UK as one of our prisoners but before that we had managed to get the information out of him that we wanted. We also retrieved some information from his aircraft. The German had come aboard very surly but left showing us a little more respect. It was really our Damage Control Team and their equipment that kept the ship alive.'

The story continues:

'By lunchtime on this sad day we had settled down to a reasonable routine. The RAF had rid the ships of Me 109s, also Me 110s, and we only received an occasional shell from some obscure source. A cold lunch was organised for us all on the bridge by the Admiral's and Captain's Stewards, who were always ready for emergencies. During the lunch the Admiral asked the Captain if much damage had been caused to his cabin. Before he could reply, the Steward said in a loud voice "Quite a bit sir, including your uniforms." Whereupon the Admiral instructed the Captain to "Get Foden to prepare the necessary forms for my Secretary. I am very sorry to hear this news." Well, I filled in the appropriate forms but could see little sign of the alleged damage; in due course, recompense was received. The Captain's Steward had done well, as usual.

He was always one step ahead of us and was rated up to Petty Officer Steward before the end of the year.

'We were at anchor off Juno Beach and gradually the landing proceeded. To our great dismay the Admiral, General and Air Marshall had no wish to go ashore. I wondered if we were going to be there forever! Meanwhile, the Germans had repositioned their flying bombs (V1s) so that they could make a nuisance of themselves.

'Our Electrical Officer found he could play havoc with this type of bomb with an electric razor! Two were required to run at any one time; he managed to find five on board, collected them all up and they were all used in rotation to throw the flying bombs off course. It was the only time I started to grow a beard! When we arrived back in Portsmouth, I reclaimed my razor and shaved properly again.'

Tom recalls a few incidents that occurred while they were at Juno Beach:

'On another occasion while we were lying there at this landing I was sunning myself on deck and noticed a merchant ship rather too close to us, looking like it was going to hit us. We let our anchor go a bit but the tide had taken hold of this other ship and he hit us just forward of the bridge. We had fortunately put some fenders out and he did not damage any of our plates. The Admiral was on the deck by then and told the merchant ship's captain that he had never seen such a terrible example of seamanship in his life. It was a light, single-screw ship and it had been picked up by the tide. It could have been a very, very serious incident, really.'

Bulolo was moored off the Normandy Coast for twenty-six days after D-Day and was hit, along with other types of bombs, by a 250 pound bomb.

'The other little incident was when Captain Kershaw saw, with dismay, the number of motor vehicles for senior officers that we carried in the forward well deck. There were eight cars there. The Captain mentioned this to the Admiral while partaking of a drink and all present suggested that Captain Kershaw should have one as well. Well, there were no spare cars aboard, so he asked me to go ashore in a landing craft with the ship's Jeep, and another LCI behind me, and find a suitable staff car for him. I asked him where I would "acquire" this car. He said that was up to me but suggested that there were some in the square in Bayeux! He assigned me to pick out the best and arranged with the Engineer Commander that Lieutenant Graham Barton-Hilton should accompany me in case there was any technical work to be done. He suggested that I take a battery with me as well, in case the battery on the chosen vehicle had been stolen. I went to the Chief-of-Staff of the Army for my pass to go ashore and he suggested that I show it very quickly or people would think that I was up to mischief and I could be shot!

'We managed to get to the square in Bayeux and there were staff cars everywhere, lots of Ford Pilots made in Antwerp with no keys in them. Graham soon managed to find a way to start one of the cars and worked the steering that had been locked with the original key and we used our spare battery to get it started. The soldiers who were hanging around were becoming increasingly interested in our activity but we weren't really very happy about the French there, who were showing an interest, too. A dairy was open nearby. I had some Camel cigarettes and went in to speak to someone to get some reassurance that they wouldn't turn on us. The lady said her husband was part of the Resistance. She called over this chap who said that we were doing okay. I gave him some cigarettes. Well, you would think I had given him gold. The lady in the dairy opened the fridge; I had never seen so many camembert cheeses in all my life. She let us take two hundred, I put them in the back of the Jeep and gave her the rest of the cigarettes that I had. When we got back the Catering Officer almost fell on the floor with happiness. However, I had to tell him that they weren't all for him. I had to inform the Captain about them and he suggested that all ninety officers should have one each. He would keep ten and I could have five! The Admiral had a fair portion of these cheeses, too, but that seemed a little unnecessary as he was going ashore and didn't really need them. The rest went to the Catering Officer, so everyone got some in the end.

'Anyway, back to the scene in Bayeux. I drove the Jeep and Graham drove the Ford Pilot. We were let through the check-points and arrived back at the beach. You could actually drive to the water as the nets were all down and the beach was in a tidy state. We picked the time just right for the tide being in and the LCIs were there waiting for us. So we loaded the Ford Pilot on, not very easily, the Jeep was a lot easier. We went astern with the Landing Craft, quietly turned them around and went back to the ship. We hoisted the nets up without much problem and the 'new' car was immediately put in the garage on board, out of sight. Then when we had the car safely in the hold we all had a sherry with the Captain. We could have had a bit of trouble with this particular car when we drove it into Bristol one evening; the number we had given it turned out to be the same as the one on the Naval Patrol vehicle that was behind us outside the Mauretania Restaurant in Park Street, Bristol! Luckily, for all concerned, it was not spotted.'

At this point it seems they were ready to go back to the UK:

'At last, we were ready to go back to England. There was a party for the "high ups." The Admiral and General were going ashore the very next day, and also the Air Marshall. We had a lot to thank the Air Marshall for; he made our lives reasonable without having a lot of enemy aircraft around us and when they had a go at us, up came the Spitfires.

'Well, back in Portsmouth I was only there for a day or two. We were sent off to Gare Loch on the Clyde and I managed to get my little MG on to *Bulolo*. By then we had a fairly well established lot of transport on board - Jeeps, staff cars and lots more, so it was pretty easy to just put another car on board. After a day or so at Gare Loch, it was getting boring and we were informed that we could have some shore leave.

'Lieutenant Robert Ellis-Brown (the South African chap) had said that he liked my MG and thought he might get early release; over a gin or two he made me a great offer. I realised he was serious and soon accepted, and he immediately paid me a cheque for the car. As it went ashore, it was only left for me to give him the car registration book and that was that. I tried to give him some advice on how to look after the MG, but he didn't take it. He took a WREN out a few nights later and one of the stones on a rough track went through the sump; he took no notice of the pressure gauge and it just seized up solid. He did get it going again, but it was never the same. After that, he soon left and I don't know what happened to the car - or to him.'

Meanwhile, shore leave!

'The Captain had already decided that he was going to be off fairly early, and left the ship in the capable hands of the Commander. We had been given two weeks leave and before he left the Captain said he didn't want anyone mucking around with his car while he was away. Well, only Graham Barton-Hilton and myself were allowed to use it. All I had to do was take the Captain to the Glasgow Railway Station, which I did. Well, it wasn't many days until the Commander said that he had his girlfriend coming up and wanted to borrow the Captain's car. He kept on and on at me until I let him have the car. He used it quite a bit with this girl friend and one day, it was early evening, the Captain arrived back early, came in on the train to Helensburgh and saw the Commander driving his girl friend in his very own car. We had been well and truly caught! He had come early because there were some new secret orders which had to be actioned immediately.

'I didn't know what to say for a couple of days. Kershaw said he realised it must have been difficult for me but suggested that the incident should be a lesson to me. He pointed out that there would be times when I would have to make these kind of decisions in the future. How true.'

Tom talks about Gare Loch:

'In Gare Loch we did a lot of sailing and watching the hills each side of us by telescope! On one side, we used to watch a red haired gentleman with an impressive red beard. He came up every evening with a new lady and there and then would perform upon the chosen lady. It was with such regularity that I am afraid we were unashamedly envious.

'I met a girl while I was up there, her father had a tumble-down house near Clynder and I used to try and see a fair bit of her, but it was difficult as I didn't have a car then. Margaret Birrell was her name and she had a sister as well. Two or three of us used to go up to the Birrell house when we could and sit in the kitchen without any nonsense. It was jolly good fun.'

While they were in that location, Tom was to lose another Captain:

'Captain Kershaw called for me one day. He had been promoted to some big Command Operations place, and told me the ship was going back to Southampton and he planned to attend the first of the Refit Conferences to prepare the ship for the Pacific. I needed to get the documentation ready for the new Captain, who he thought would be a pretty senior RNR

Captain as these chaps needed as much sea-going experience as possible before the end of the war. I was heavy-hearted when I left his cabin, for it was to be the end of a wonderful period of my life. We returned to Southampton where the conference was going to be held, virtually straight away. The refit was going to take about six weeks and then we would be off to the Pacific.

'There were lots and lots of personnel changes. I thought I might go then, but the Admiralty in their wisdom suggested I stay on to keep continuity on board the ship. The new Captain, A.A. Martin, RNR, didn't show up 'til later, but I had already received some good reports about him. He had been the Harbourmaster at Freetown, Sierra Leone, before the war.

'I got all my work up to date. The Commander was still on board and we had a lot of fun while hanging around. We put up with all the refit business and I was glad that I stayed. I bought a J2 MG for about £40, a lot of money, then. I started to use it quite a bit and life was okay. I used to see my girl-friend, June Monkhouse, to whom I had become engaged. She was an actress and got a job with the Royal Shakespeare Company, so I used to go up to Stratford-on-Avon most weekends. Sadly, we gave up this engagement as we found out that we weren't temperamentally suited. I found it so hard to follow her around when she started touring and she was glad when we broke up as well, as neither of us was really what the other wanted as a life companion. We still keep in touch after all these years.'

Tom remembers one particular occasion with June:

'My family had a Samoyed dog called Boris who used to come out in my MG. People used to ask me who was driving the car, me or Boris? I used to take him up to the Downs when I was home on leave. One afternoon I had left June with Boris for a short time and another dog, an Alsatian, went for him, not realising that he didn't really have a chance against Boris. When I got there they seemed to be getting more and more into each other, and I wasn't keen on separating them. I found some gloves and just as I was about to get to grips with the problem a woman behind me asked who was going to deal with this fracas. I suggested the owner should; she obviously meant that that should be me! I did separate them and found the Alsatian was in a bit of a mess really. She immediately started on me again, asking who was going to pay for the vet bill. I put the Alsatian in my car and took him down to a jolly good vet I knew who sorted him out, at the expense of a £20 note. The lady didn't even apologise, or thank me for sorting the matter out. I realised the moral to all of this was that I should have got on and separated them straight away!'

Back to *Bulolo*:

'The ship's refit was completed, it was just the last word in Technology. We now had even more tape recorders on the ship. Most conversations were taped. We had all sorts of radio, radar, equipment for night fighters, and equipment for shooting down Japanese planes at night. Captain Martin arrived; we got on well from the start. I thought I was very lucky to have such a good replacement for Kershaw. We moved up to the Tail of the Bank, Scotland, to join the convoy that was going out to Trincomalee.

'The Escort for this Convoy was unbelievable, I had never seen so many aircraft carriers in all my life. Trincomalee is on the East coast of Sri Lanka (Ceylon), one of the best harbours in the World. We lost one of the best and most wanted merchant ships on the way; she caught fire and we couldn't put the fire out and that was the end of that one.

'We carried out one or two exercises off the coast of Trincomalee and it became apparent to me that the efficiency of our previous landings was not coming to the foreground.

We had all these carriers with Spitfires, destroyers, mine sweepers and others and it was obvious that we weren't far off sailing. Captain Martin was the senior captain and he and I went to all the meetings and found that the landing was going to be at Port Swettenham (Pelabohan Kelang, Malaysian Peninsular) not far from Singapore - actually it is closer to Kuala Lumpur. It seemed a fairly easy landing. We were assured that it had been very heavily surveyed by submarine but this was not so.

'Anyway, the day came when we sailed. I sailed with a heavy heart, as I was concerned about our luck running out and knew that we couldn't possibly be lucky enough where the Japanese were concerned, as they were devils. I wrote a long letter to my mother and to a girlfriend I had latched on to when I was last home. When we had been at sea for about thirty-six hours messages kept coming in and I had a whole heap of things to go through with the Captain. Then on 6th August 1945 as I walked past one of the loudspeakers that was giving the latest BBC News I heard about a bomb that had been dropped on Hiroshima. We all talked about it afterwards and thought that it must be this Atomic Bomb thing.

'We heard about another bomb thirty-six hours before it was the 'H' Hour to our landing. And another bomb was threatened for Tokyo. Later that day the Emperor decided to call it a day and surrendered, but it wasn't made clear if his Armed Forces would go along with this decision. However, the mood on board the ship was pretty celebratory. That evening we heard that the Japanese Army, Airforce and Navy had all surrendered.

'We heard that the landing was to go ahead but no offensive measures were to be carried out unless the Japanese gave us trouble. That was just as well as the beach was a quagmire. All the equipment, tanks, lorries, jeeps got stuck in mud - and then the Japanese got their tractors and pulled us out! It was obvious that the Emperor's word had worked, for they came and shook our hands and saluted. A lot of them gave us their swords. I nicked one and kept it in my cabin for a few days but then it was stolen from me. The beaches were soon netted without too much problem and the rest of the equipment could be got off.'

They moved on to Singapore:

'Admiral Lord Louis Mountbatten accepted the surrender from the Japanese Commander-in-Chief. I went with Graham and one or two of the new officers to watch this great spectacle, and took some photos. The Japanese were on their best behaviour and we soon found ourselves berthed alongside Lord Louis's cruiser, where he flew his flag. When the cruiser had to leave, *Bulolo* flew it for him.

'I had lost my immediate boss, the Supply Officer Mike Hutton, who was wanted very urgently by the P & O. He left us, recommending me for his job. Captain Martin read my reports and said that my assistant could take on my jobs and I could get on with being the Supply Officer. That meant that at some ridiculous age I was a Lieutenant-Commander. The Admiralty didn't agree and sent someone else out. Unfortunately he was not well received and packed off back and I was then appointed.

'This was when Lord Louis flew his flag on *Bulolo* and he wanted to do a lot of entertaining on board ship. He sent for me and that very evening had decided he wanted to give a dinner, and so the Catering Officer and I set to and produced a pleasant meal and a good evening was had by all. Lord Louis was very like Captain Kershaw but it took a lot more to please him. We did everything right and he had just come from another ship where he hadn't been looked after very well, so that helped us a great deal.

'What happened to the huge Task Force? No-one was certain what the Japanese would do next so everyone had to go to their designated landings. The Emperor's word meant that the Japanese were to put up no resistance at all. They were true to their word and helped us, doing all sorts of tasks. What was rather sad was to see the British prisoners out of Changi Jail going on to the hospital ships. They looked just terrible, and it took a while for them to chirp up a bit. They were sent in various troop ships back to the UK or to India, where they could receive better treatment. Some did not survive.

'We were in Singapore for quite a while. I latched on to a young Chinese chap, Martin Lee, whose father had the main photographic shop there. He didn't waste any time after the surrender in getting the shop going and started to do business again. He invited us to his house, which had been full of Japanese previously; the Chinese family (the Lees) had been forced to live in the garden in a hut. But they came back into the house and soon enough we were able to get the refrigerator going again. Martin told me that he had a T Type MG before the war, but had decided to bury it so that the Japanese couldn't use it! Captain Martin was very good and wanted to keep the sailors occupied so I mustered up a dozen sailors with picks and shovels to unearth this car, which was buried about six or seven feet deep. We got it out, most of it fine. Only some small parts were damaged by insects but even the hood was intact. My chum Graham got it going and we used it quite a bit while the *Bulolo* remained there.'

Tom lets us know of activities going on around them:

'In the Dutch East Indies, especially, there was a lot of activity going on. The local people had turned on the Dutch and so we were ordered to Surabaya to bring back any women and children we could carry. We did not have any charts for this area as we were not really expecting to go there. Having frightened the locals with our machine guns, fired by the Marines on board, we embarked about 700 personnel - ladies, children and old people. They had some terrible stories to tell. We went back for another load and managed to get away on both trips without any loss of life.

'After the surrender ceremony at Singapore, things rapidly began to return to normal. We helped a lot with the reopening of the radio station: on a couple of nights I read the evening news bulletin in great solemnity. We also assisted in the co-ordination of shipping for a short while.

'I noticed that the P & O liner *RMS Corfu* was due in shortly. Roy Pullen, the Purser, was still on board, as far as I knew, and I thought very highly of him. As he had invited me to dinner on a couple of occasions when he was Deputy Purser in *Strathnaver*, and we were all in anchorage together in Algiers, I thought it was about time that I reciprocated, so I sent him an RPC ("Request Pleasure of Your Company") for a couple of days from then, when I knew the liner would definitely be in. You may, or may not be able to imagine, how I felt when one of our many radio personnel handed me an envelope saying, "It's not good news." It read: "Regret to inform you that Roy Pullen was killed five days ago falling down a hatch. He was in no way inebriated. All hands and passengers attended his burial at sea two days ago. We miss this very popular officer." And so do I. A product of one of our famous public schools, it seemed so unfair that after spending an active war at sea for the whole duration, this should happen. Life is not all beer and skittles.'

Tom tells us how he had a great end to the year:

'We spent a wonderful New Year at the Raffles Hotel. However, we received a nasty signal straight afterwards to return to the UK. We found that we could take passengers with us and having reported to the Sea Transport Officer that we could take about 110 service people, the wheels were set in motion. There was no problem, as there were thousands waiting to go back. We were sorry to leave young Lee and his delightful family - and the MG. We found all sorts of vegetables and other goods on board that they had given us.

'We were routed through the Suez Canal and the whole world seemed to be waiting to go through with us. We had been away well over nine months by then and everybody was ready to go home. I remember a delightful man, Jim Irish, who was the Admiralty Contractor for Port Said, Port Tewfiq (Bur Taufiq) and Alexandria. Sale Bey Salim, was his real name. He came aboard and we asked him for potatoes, oranges and other basic fruit and vegetables. While we went through the Suez Canal he said we could get off and go around the Pyramids, then be taken back to the ship and meet it again in Port Said. So I asked the Captain if that was possible and he agreed. A couple of other Lt-Comds and Graham and other personnel went with me. It was a lovely trip, the car was full of chilled fruits and other splendid foods. We got through to Port Said in good time and while we were away all the vegetables arrived onboard the ship.

'We were secured on one of the walkways at Port Said so they could load all these goods very easily. I stopped one of the trucks that were delivering to inspect the produce and underneath the top layer of good fruit and vegetables was rubbish. I soon stopped the bad stuff from getting on, spoke to Jim about it and he said that I was very clever to figure it out. But he still tried to blame the people who were delivering the goods!

'Jim said that the next day he wanted to take Captain Martin and myself to see the new mosque he was building in Port Said. He knew the Captain already and so we left the ship in the hands of the Commander (new guy), a very nice chap but not quite the same character as the previous Commander. So, Jim had a carriage and horse waiting for us. We had flowers for our lapels and went through the streets of Port Said waving at the crowds. I realised this Jim chap was really quite important. I thought that there might be a catch, after the Pyramid trip, as among these chaps, one of our fairly senior Communications chaps, a man called Molloy, had also been asked to come in this carriage, but there wasn't enough room for him, so he went in a separate car. Anyhow, we went around this Mosque and it transpired that Jim was looking for some sound-reproduction equipment. Captain Martin said we could sort him out and if he was asked later about it he would have to say that the Royal Navy had given it to him as it was very out of date and would otherwise have been scrapped. Molloy was approached to carry this out and had to write off the equipment that was going to be used and was told that Jim Irish would be up to see us the next day. Jim did approach us and by way of thanks he delivered to the ship a huge package of Turkish Delight. It was wonderful, and I wasn't the only one to enjoy it, for he had some put in the sailor's Messes as well.

'Off we went through the Mediterranean, it was frightful weather. Two or three of our ventilators were damaged and we went into Malta to have them fixed. Then we had another change of Captain. Captain Martin had to go and we then had Captain J.H. Plumer. He had been in destroyers all his life, a real Royal Navy chap. He was a very nice man but I can't say that I really took a shine to him because he seemed to expect the unexpected and he just treated the *Bulolo* as another destroyer. He did not show the ship much by way of respect and he used to throw it around a lot, but there was no real damage done. I used to hate being asked to do this, that and the other at about ten o'clock at night; e didn't seem to rate sleep very highly. As I was now the Supply Officer, some of these jobs were not really my concern, but the chap who took my place was a little too young to stand up to the Captain, so I just got on with it.

'We arrived back in the UK at Portsmouth and I went on leave. Having saved quite a bit of money I sold my J2 and bought a PB MG, made in 1936. This was thought to be the best that they had ever made. So after the leave we were sent off to Gare Loch again - a long way from civilisation. Getting there by train was pretty hard, with all the soldiers and sailors being de-mobbed and trying to get around. Anyhow, up we went and we, of course, wanted to see if the red-haired man still carried on, but it didn't seem so.

'The girl that I had been seeing up there before, she and her family were still there. I found an old Austin 7 that had been used to take luggage from Helensburgh up to some hotel in the hills, so I bought it and drove it around to Margaret's house, and with the help of her father, we rebuilt it.

'Nobody seemed to know what to do with *Bulolo*, peace was settling down very quickly and here we were with a full ship's company, ready to proceed. We thought that we might have to go off and collect troops, but it didn't happen. Once or twice we heard rumours about missions but nothing came of it and so we stayed there for quite a while. I had some very painful varicose veins removed while I was up there. I had a girl friend in Bristol still and, of course, Margaret was in Gare Loch, but she was more like a sister by then.

'We carried on doing a lot of sailing up there. The winds would come down off the hills and it was a truly great experience. We also had one or two strange Engineer Officers; they were thin on the ground. When we had to have the reliefs we knew that we were scraping the bottom of the barrel. One such chap had a father who ran the local buses. When he went ashore, he took the bus up and around the Gare Loch, it was an experience but we managed to get rid of him before he did too much damage!

'The Admiralty lost the battle to the Australians and *Bulolo* was to be returned to Australia as a liner, but before that to be converted and rebuilt at the Clyde in Glasgow by Barclay Curle, who had originally built her. It was very, very sad but I took my hat off to the Engineer Commander, Bill Monteith, who was responsible for this decision. He had been tugging away at people in the Admiralty, and politicians, of which he knew many, and as a result of the activities of the previous few years they listened to him. So we left our dear old Gare Loch and I sold my Austin 7 that I had so carefully rebuilt. I placed an advertisement in the Glasgow Echo and received many replies. Some lucky Army lieutenant had it off me. I made a considerable amount of money at the time, £99; I had only given £10 or £15 for it originally.

'So off we went up the Clyde to Glasgow. We were all due to be paid-off fairly soon before Christmas in 1946 and we got to the yard where the ship was going to be rebuilt. I was due to leave the following day and we were going to lower the White Ensign in the morning and raise the Red Australian Ensign. Before we went there was a lot of redistribution of equipment, the Communications Officer saying that the priceless parts would be ripped out, the secret stuff would be burned and the rest would just go in some ship and be dumped in mid-Atlantic. I got a lovely radio receiver called a B 28, a godsend to me for a few days 'til I left the ship, when the Chief Engineer asked me to give it back to him. Someone pinched it off him the very next day! The Chief Engineer had been really looking forward to using this radio while he supervised the refit.'

Skipping a few years, British ships were going to Suez and Alexandria during the 'crisis' of 1956:

'The Admiral said, at the time, quite unashamedly, that if we still had *Bulolo* he would have been in Cairo before he had instructions to stop. But the communications were not so good and so we did not get to Cairo.'

*

Chapter 6
From RNR to RN on
HMS Anson
December 1946 to November 1948

'Some chum in Bristol asked me to pick up on my way back from Glasgow an Alvis 1250 that he had bought. I managed to get some petrol and drove it, but it was pretty slow and on the way I had to go to Liverpool to *HMS Mersey* to 'sign off', as we had been temporarily assigned to that ship after coming off *Bulolo*. Bill Monteith was with me and I had to drop him at the station at Liverpool; he went back to Glasgow and we had a sad parting as we had been together for a long time.

'As soon as I arrived home I took my PB MG out of the garage in Queens court and tidied it up, ready to take it on board *HMS Anson*, to which I had been appointed as Deputy Supply Officer. I also had to go to London to see the guy who was doing the appointing of RNR Officers, as I had been offered a temporary RN commission and I had to sign various documents. I found out that the head of this part of the organisation was Commodore Sir Richard Harrison, who had been the Captain of *RMS Stratheden* when I had served in her. He remembered me but I couldn't take up his offer of lunch as my train was leaving pretty soon. He was ending his war career and going back to Portsmouth to his farm.

'I went back to Bristol and spent a few days at home, saw my girl friend and prepared myself for *HMS Anson*. I was to serve on a battleship, so I had my uniforms all cleaned and my car cleaned and serviced and the day came when I went to Portland Harbour. Unfortunately, it started to snow and by the time I had managed to get the car ready the snow was settling.

I realised that the trip over the Mendips was going to be pretty tricky. The coach from Bristol to Weymouth was just in front of me. It had chains on its wheels and I thought it might be able to plough a way through for me, so I stuck behind it and eventually we got down to Dorchester, where the snow was considerably less from there on to Weymouth. I left my car in a garage and went by taxi to the harbour to meet the liberty boat to take me to the battleship. I was shown my cabin, it was like a dog hutch! I met Commander Hardy RN and Captain Markham Eveleigh RN; they were both real gentlemen. I had come to quite a new turn in my life. No rubbishy officers here! It was pretty refreshing.

'As I said, I was appointed to the position of Stores and Deputy Supply Officer. The Supply Officer was a chap called Norman Edgar Denning. He contracted influenza and so on that very first night he called me in and said he wouldn't be able to come on board for at least ten days. He wanted me to close the Year End accounts and I really had to agree. Myself and a few junior officers whom I persuaded to stay up, did so and we got it done.

'It was very rewarding work on this ship and I stayed with her for about two years. It wasn't long before I got to know everyone, including a lovely Anglican padre called Bernard Beasley and an even more interesting Roman Catholic padre, Michael Barry. Michael was an absolute must for his job; everyone on board thought a lot of him and Bernard was also highly thought of, as well. Bernard had a married quarter on land and let Michael leave his car there.'

Tom talks of life at Portland:

'The ship was based in Portland and we spent a lot of the time swinging at anchor, and as a result we had numerous invitations from various bodies in the area. One of these was the 'Daughters of Dorset.' They had a lovely roadhouse party near to Dorchester and I soon met a girl that I thought very highly of. Michael Barry, without his dog collar, used to come, too, and used to attract a lot of attention! The girls didn't believe him when they asked him what he did; they used to say he must be the Deputy Head of the Royal Marines as he was much too young to be a padre! He used to invite them to the Sunday cinema on board, having first received permission from our Commander, and they were thunderstruck when they saw Michael in the uniform of a padre. Very sadly, when Michael left us he went to Malaya to one of the Royal Marine Commando units and was ambushed in a patrol of eight people. Seven of them, including Michael, were killed. It was a terrible tragedy.'

Tom remembers incidents between Michael and Bernard:

'Bernard Beasley used to lie and say to Michael that he could have any of his parishioners as long as they were all good Christians. Another trick Michael tried was that he realised that sailors are not stupid, and anything they can do to get another quarter or half an hour in their hammocks in the morning, the better. They realised that if they became Roman Catholic they didn't have to go to the Roll Call first thing in the morning! When Bernard and Michael talked about this, Bernard realised he was loosing some of his group, but Michael wasn't getting any more converts at his service, either. These sailors were just saying they had converted to the Roman Catholic faith. The Captain heard of this and decided he was going to put an end to it all. He spoke to the whole ship, saying that all the Roman Catholics could get together the following week at 7 o'clock each morning and have a jolly good sing-song. There was a queue of people wishing to return to Bernard! Michael Barry also, somehow, managed to persuade Cardinal Griffin to spend three days with the ship. Admiral Harold Hickley, the Flag Officer, Training Squadron, entered into this scheme also, and thought it would be jolly good to have the Cardinal on board. Well, anyway, while he was on board he came into the wardroom and had a gin or two and I spoke to him myself. He asked me very courteously what was my position in the ship and after I told him, he told me a lovely story that happened at the end of the First World War, while he was in the *Iron Duke*, where he was serving as a Stores Assistant. They had to throw all the remaining stores over the side and some flares were sent over by mistake; somehow they ignited and smoked and people thought they were in severe distress! He let on that that incident rather made his mind up to join the priesthood! I was glad to hear all of this, especially as we were about to sort out our supplies of flares the very next day!'

Tom tells us a little about the Supply Officer, who joined the ship after his bout of influenza:

'The Supply Officer, Norman Edgar Denning had received many decorations but had done very little sea-time as far as I could learn. He was, however, concerned with what was going on at Bletchley Park and it seemed that he had had rather a lot to do with the de-coding, as he had been the Deputy Head of the organisation at Bletchley at some time. He was old before his years. He must have been right in the thick of it all, or so I thought, with the *Bismark* and the *Hood*. He was a dedicated man and I was very fortunate to be his deputy. We all made sure that we carried out our tasks with the same diligence that he showed. He knew that I had known about D-day and had been sworn to secrecy way before the news broke, and he spent some time confiding in me what had happened for him, knowing that I wouldn't tell anyone.

'We had so many chaps like Denning to thank for many things that happened during the war. We also had a lot of fun. On one occasion, when we had to go to see the Staff Supply

Officer in Portsmouth, Denning suggested that we should go in my car. We had a wonderful day and we stopped at a pub and he really let his hair down. I think we had just heard that he had been promoted to Captain and would be leaving us shortly. I was very sorry to hear that he had died recently.'

Tom talks about *HMS Anson*:

'We were the Flagship of the Training Squadron and carried out many forays in seamanship, along with the *Howe* and various other ships that turned up in Portland Harbour at the time. We had to be very cost-conscious and it cost a fortune to carry out these forays, so we didn't do that many. We did go to Torquay quite often, however. Mr Chapman, the owner of the Imperial Hotel, was very keen on entertaining the Navy. It was a lovely hotel and we used to enjoy the cocktail parties that were laid on for us. On other trips we sometimes went to Falmouth and I remember the only time I went there it was snowing ashore. This made it very hard work, it being such a dreadful day. Before the ship entered harbour Admiral Hickling called the navigator, Tony Griffin, (he later became First Sea Lord) to talk to him about entering Falmouth. The Admiral was very anxious to arrive; the navigator said that the Admiral had told him that he was no good if he couldn't take this damn ship almost up to St Mawes.'

Tom reminds us, it was blowing very hard:

'Tony had the added pressure that he was going to get engaged to the Admiral's daughter! He got us in okay, it was nail-biting stuff but we managed to anchor in the harbour safely. I think Tony Griffin would have slept well that night. Tony became a Lieutenant-Commander soon after that and then continued being promoted throughout his naval career. He was a very dedicated chap and a charming man at the same time.'

While with this lovely ship, Tom enjoyed some fine weather:

'During the last summer that I was in *Anson*, we sailed around the UK. We stopped at Wick, the Orkneys, Shetlands, Skye, and various other islands in those parts. We anchored off Skye and saw Mrs Macleod of Macleod; she owned Skye and made us very welcome when we stayed there. The Royal Marines band played 'Over the Sea to Skye' as we entered the anchorage. It was very moving. Then we went off to Glasgow. We anchored there for a few days.

'One of the Officers on board told me that *Bulolo* was in the harbour! Well, I couldn't wait to see her. She looked beautiful in the colours of the Burns Philip Line, destined for the service from Sydney to New Guinea. She still had the same Chief Engineer, Bill Monteith. I called him up on Channel 16 and told him that he had made a marvellous job of her. He, in turn, said that every cabin was taken with people emigrating.

'The *Queen Elizabeth* was also there and we saw her go out on her first peacetime voyage. It was sad to see *Bulolo* go and that evening when I had dinner with the Admiral, Tony Griffin and Tom Briggs (who went to *Berkeley Castle* soon after) the Admiral asked me about life on *Bulolo*. He realised that some of this information was secret and thought how sad it was that we had lost such a good communications ship, especially when we needed one so badly. We all knew that it was such a shame that it had gone to trade. Tony Griffin married the Admiral's daughter shortly after that.

'One time or another we had a nice dance on deck and were honoured to have their Majesties the King and Queen, with the Royal Princesses, Elizabeth and Margaret, to one of the evenings when we were entertaining on the Clyde. From the Clyde we went to Liverpool, and then to Swansea. Swansea wasn't bad, we were getting closer to Bristol, to home for me.

Unfortunately, we got mixed up with the *Devonia*, one of the ferries that ran from Swansea to Ilfracombe. Tony Griffin told them in no uncertain terms that they were too close! Danger was averted. From that part of the coast we then went around to Torquay, and then back to Portland for our summer leave.'

Whilst still aboard, Tom remembers some sad news:

'Before I left *Anson*, I had a little sadness from home. A lady called Nicholls, my mother's best friend, became very ill and she knew that she wouldn't last very long. So I went to see 'Auntie Kate', who had been a dear to my mother and also to me. She had a lovely house in North Somerset. She had plenty of money and wine and if I ever took a girlfriend down there we were well looked after. She told me that nobody could live forever and that when she was going to fade away, I would soon find out that I hadn't been left out.'

Tom returns after this visit:

'I went back on board and were starting to take our RNVR and RNR Officers for their two weeks training, so we were fairly busy. One of the chaps we trained was called Bradstock, the Managing Director of University Motors in London, the MG distributors. He knew that I was pretty keen on MGs and I told him one evening about Auntie Kate and that I was probably going to receive some money. He suggested that I might need a new MG and, of course, I thought that I would have to pay well over the odds for it, but he offered to find me a new TD for the proper purchase price, nothing more than that. He got on to it straight away when he went ashore, and true to his word he earmarked one for me, letting me know that it would probably take about six months.'

The story continues:

'Auntie Kate died and I went to the captain to ask for some time off but it was right in the middle of the first NATO war exercise. He said that it was impossible and that I could just send a note, so that is what I did. We got back from the NATO exercise two days later and I had a shore call allocated for 6 o'clock that evening. I phoned my mother and asked how things had gone with the funeral. She wasn't very forthcoming, obviously upset that I had not had time to attend the funeral; however, she did tell me that I hadn't received a penny! Every penny had been given to the Salvation Army! We found out that some Salvation Army chap had been to see Auntie Kate and talked her into altering her Will fairly late on. I was rather devastated, as you can imagine, especially as I thought that I was going to be coming into quite a bit of money. Serves me right really! Well, the next weekend, I went to Auntie Kate's house to see what was left. I took some tyres and a can of petrol and few bits and bobs that were hanging around. I then had a jolly good look around the wine cellar and found some good South African wine and some whisky. There was another chap down there and we started a conversation, as we both wanted to know why the other was there, really. There had been some searchlights at the house during the war, so I thought he must be there in connection with that. How wrong can one be: he was the Salvation Army Audit Officer! Thankfully, he let me take whatever I wanted, so I loaded it all in the car before he audited it. He told me that Auntie Kate's money would be well spent over the years and would be used very carefully.

'So I went off very disgruntled, back to *Anson*. As the years have ticked by, I have seen the work of the Salvation Army - it was better they were left the money! But I did get a lovely radio from Auntie Kate, as well.

'At about the same time I received a note from people called the Appointers at the Admiralty to tell me that at the end of that year I would be re-appointed. I had a lot of fun for the rest of that year and had a lovely girl friend then. Nearly married her, but I was re-appointed and went off and when I got back she had married an Army officer!

'One of the last things that happened while I was still serving in *Anson* involved one of our cooks. This man went and filled in some chappy at a pub in Weymouth, tried to knife him, and I went with him to see the Judge to try and smooth things over. He wanted to give the cook five years, and he did! I went back to the ship rather sad; it seemed a pretty hard sentence. You couldn't get so much reduction in those days, I think he had to do at least three years.

'Then it was my time to leave. My relief arrived and he must have been a good chap for he was promoted within nine months of taking over my job. I had a great report from the captain and took some well-earned leave. I thought I was going to be appointed to the Admiral's staff in Gibraltar but then I heard I was going to be the Stores Officer at the Reserve Fleet, which didn't pleased me at all.'

*

Chapter 7
Stone Frigates
December 1948 to April 1955

'I took leave in November, December and part of January as well. I had quite a lot of fun while I was at home and my mother asked me if I would like to have a cocktail party before I went back, which was very kind of her; and, of course, I said that I would love a party. Well, it wasn't all going to plan really, on the evening. We were rather enjoying ourselves and one of the girls that I had invited managed to acquire hold of one of my mother's priceless small chairs and threw it out of the window, down to the street below, narrowly missing someone who was passing. Her boyfriend was in the British Overseas Airways Corporation (BOAC) based at Whitchurch, Bristol, and he very kindly found a chair similar in an antique shop in Bristol and replaced it. He didn't stay with BOAC; for some reason they kept changing the planes that they were flying. Anyway, he was rather cross with his girl friend, who had rather a sore part of her anatomy as a result of his actions. I had an awful time waiting for this replacement chair!'

Well, soon after that, Tom returned to work:

'At Harwich it was snowing, it was mid-January of 1949 and I had a terrible trip up. By then, telephoning long distances was not difficult and I had found out from the chap I was relieving that there was a warehouse on the quay where I could leave my car, which I did, and then took the liberty boat from there to the ship. The Destroyer Depot Ship, *Tyne*, was much better than I imagined and had beautiful accommodation, almost up to *Bulolo* standard. I was lucky to have a really nice Captain as well, Johnny Lee-Barber, a great destroyer captain.

He was very interested in sailing and we had a lovely windfall yacht from the Germans. It was called *Flandern*, and with my love of sailing I very quickly became the chap who ran this little yacht. We all had a good time with her. I learnt a very great deal sailing *Flandern*.'

Recounting the general feeling:

'The overall atmosphere in the *Tyne* was one of going back, not forward, as the Admiralty were relocating a lot of dead wood as they didn't know where to put people. It was very sad from the point of view of everything that we had all worked for.'

However, work was plentiful for Tom on the *Tyne*:

'The minesweepers were all being brought up-to-date, and so we were working against the clock to get them ready for sea. There were an immense number of gears, anchors, radios, cables and other pieces of equipment needing to be refitted. You had to have a good background knowledge for this. Luckily, I had acquired this on board *Anson*. Some of these minesweepers were left in a terrible state. We managed to modernise one after another of them, like a treadmill. We kept to our target dates; it was very interesting but not a terribly eventful period of my life, workwise.

'I don't like the East Coast. It is cold in winter and there is not a lot of sun in summer. To make amends for all this hard work and being stuck on this part of the coast, therefore, in that first year we had a big regatta to keep spirits up! Well, I and my crew won the cup for the Pulling Regatta. I was thrown over the side of the boat when we won, as is traditionally done.

'Sadly, *Tyne* was brought forward, she was going to Korea and I was sent to the *Woolwich*. We had to get the *Woolwich* up to scratch just in case she was needed as well. She went to the Far East and we then had the *Dodman Point*, a destroyer Depot Ship. She was a ship the Navy had got hold of during the war and had been rebuilt for her present role. We had a nice Captain, J.C. Stopford, pretty senior in age and a very good RN Captain. There was a lot of work to be done as all these ships had to be re-commissioned quickly ready to go East.

'Meanwhile, I was going to be relocated, too. I was kidded into thinking it was going to be Gibraltar but it was really the RN Air Station at Lossiemouth. I was not sorry to leave Harwich really, and JB 3966, my MG, and I went off to Bristol on leave. This leave took me over the Christmas of 1951 into January 1952, and it was in the New Year that I went off to Lossiemouth. It could take up to two days in a car like that and at the end of the first day I found myself in Stirling, in heavy snow and it was very heavy going thereafter. An articulated lorry full of Naval stores was in front of me on the second day and I just followed in his tracks. We got on quite well. He had a big urn of tea on board and every time this little convoy stopped he gave me a cup of tea. He told me that the weather we were having was particularly good! He was a driver for the Naval Air Station and I would see more of him, later on, for I would be his boss!'

Tom arrived at Lossiemouth, not expecting what was to come:

'My Commander at Lossiemouth was John Ellerton, who had been the C-in-C's secretary in *Bulolo* for the Algiers landing. Yet again, he was sick on my arrival and I had to get on with the job straight away. This was rather daunting as it was a very large station there. Commander Ellerton was fairly close to being made Captain, so it was a hefty job that I was going into anyway, now, without any help.

'One of the problems I had to sort out when I arrived was the theft of a lot of petrol which was, unfairly, being blamed on my Department. Later it was found to be a local scrap dealer who managed to redirect the supply during the leave period on the base. Luckily, when Commander Ellerton got back off his sick leave everything settled down into a good routine.'

Life at Lossiemouth was looking up:

'I wasn't entirely inexperienced but it is the real thing that makes the job and we had a lot of young chaps and some WREN officers at the station as well. Having been starved of female company for a long time in my naval career I found this rather fun. The Mother Superior, the Senior WREN, was a little awe-inspiring but us chaps used to lead her an awful dance. There was one girl, Peggy Warner (of the travel family) who was quite beautiful. As she lived in Tewkesbury, she accepted a lift off me when we went on Easter leave, which upset some of the chaps at the Station. On this trip we stopped to help someone who had broken down and while my attention was elsewhere some kind soul put a matchstick in one of my tyre valves, making it gently go down. I had to stop to keep pumping it up. I had invited Peggy to my home but my mother was hopping mad and was not going to allow it at all, so I had to tell Peggy that mother had 'flu. She didn't believe me, but she didn't mind too much, either.

'Then everyone returned for the summer, not a real summer as I knew it, I had an awful cabin, it was really cold. The Steward provided coal and wood for the fire, but I had bought an electric stove in Elgin some time before and one night had a little incident when a shirt of mine went up in flames. I had been airing it too closely to the fire and the Fire Brigade arrived to put it out. As I had to sleep in the cabin that night the Commander found it rather amusing. I was worried that I was going to be court-martialled, but it was not to be and I continued in that cabin until it was redecorated.

'I then managed to persuade the Commander to allocate myself and the Deputy Electrical Officer, Gillie Potter, a little hut, with all sorts of rooms, and so we had a room each as well as a sitting room and a dining room, and it was very much better. We were able to park our cars outside the hut and for the early 1950's it really was luxury.

'I hadn't been in the hut very long when the phone rang and the Police in Elgin were letting me know that the Supply Commander had been in an accident and would probably be returned to the sick bay at the Station from Elgin hospital. However, the hospital rang in the night and asked me to call the Commander's wife and let her know. I didn't call her 'til the early morning. She took it very philosophically. I spoke to the Surgeon Commander and who told me he was going to the civilian hospital to see if the Commander could be moved back to the Sick Bay. He was moved, but he was only semi-conscious, and asked me to look after Pilot, his black Labrador. When I got through to his wife, she was, obviously, concerned and I said I would keep her informed.

'It was obvious that the Commander would not return to work for at least a month, so I was made up to Acting Commander - and had to look after Pilot! Pilot used to walk around the stores with me and one day got locked into this huge building for a whole afternoon. When he was retrieved in the evening he was jolly happy. It seemed that he had eaten a whole cat during the afternoon, except for the claws, which we found! Pilot was now the king of this huge building. He had never been friendly with the cat. He was known from then on as "the cat-eating dog"!'

Antics at Lossiemouth continued:

'On another occasion the Control Tower informed us that they were in contact with an American passenger plane which had lost one of its engines and could possibly loose another. It would have to come to a diversion airfield: in other words, they were on their way to us at Lossiemouth. We were put to

"Action Stations", with the Padre warned to be on hand. We had supplies and a good long runway, and additional lighting was found to place on it. My chum, Gillie Potter, was expected to set it all up. I was changing the plugs on my MG in the garage at the time and Gillie was under an Austin 10 putting in some new big ends. Of course Action Stations meant we *had* to move immediately but Gillie seemed in no hurry and after about ten minutes someone from the Control Tower sent a rating to come and collect Gillie. He did something with the lighting and got the new lights going at least a quarter of an hour before the American plane was sighted! The plane was now down to two engines but managed to land with a bit of a jolt and the sound of metal scraping along the runway. It didn't catch fire, as we had placed a curtain of foam along the runway. We welcomed the sixty passengers warmly and took care of them, and when they went on their way they were very grateful for the treatment that they had received. It turned out, in fact, to be a very successful interlude all round: the American pilot did a good job in getting her down and we did well in looking after all the passengers.'

On a much lighter subject, Tom tells us of the sailing that he experienced there:

'Also at Lossiemouth we did some super sailing at a little harbour called Findhorn. We used to take off each weekend. I was the Boat Officer, so I saw to it that we got some decent dinghies from the Naval Stores, and a couple of whalers. There was a Yacht Club at Findhorn where we occasionally stayed for supper, and in the end they made most of us who sailed Honorary Members. There was also a strange place close by to the Club, a sort of Faith-Healing haven where other activities were also carried out. The Mother Superior for the WRENs placed it out of bounds to them but my wife tells me it was perfectly okay and would have done the WRENs some good!

'We had our moments sailing over a sand bar which was pretty dangerous. Two victims had died just before I arrived and when I took over the responsibility for the sailing I was determined that this should not happen again. The bar was placed out of bounds and the only time we went over it to the other side of the loch was to a Regatta there, when we were using one of the whalers. It took about twelve hours to cross the loch, so we had to stay overnight - it was pretty cold there - and then come back. We came second in our race in this whaler, which wasn't bad at all.

'We were very close to Gordonstoun, which the Prince of Wales was attending. They did a lot of sailing at that well-run establishment, which seemed to have some good ideals. There were a lot of nice young gentleman being brought up there; some of them used to come around to the station, where we tried to persuade them to join the Navy. As well as the Prince of Wales, the Duke of Edinburgh had been there in his time. It made men of these people.'

There were sad times at this period in Tom's life, as well:

'When I was at Lossiemouth my father and my stepfather both died within a couple of months of each other. I was a little more solvent as a result of these sad happenings and I bought myself a TC MG which really almost transformed my existence. I got rid of the JB 3966 and bought this new car from Windmill and Lewis in Clifton; they took the old JB in part exchange and the new one was about £500, so it was a good deal, all in all!

'The TC MG really flew. When it came to leaving Lossie-mouth I nearly ruined this lovely car driving through snow in it for over four hundred miles. But, in the meantime, it was great fun and it commanded quite a bit of attention. My days in drawing pay as an Acting Commander lasted for about four months and as I looked after Pilot for almost all that time we became good chums. He used to sit in the front of my cars with me when I drove about, and he was always first into the yacht when we went sailing.

'Pilot, by now, had learnt a special trick. One of his great feats of seamanship was to gnaw through the whaler's main halyard when we were in the middle of a sailing race, making us look like a lot of ghosts floundering around. We had a new Supply Commander then, a chap called Gar Mowl, who took over from Ellerton before I left the Station.

'One of the major events while I was at Lossiemouth was for me to attend for an interview, in uniform, to decide if I was going to be given a permanent commission. I didn't think that I would ever get it as they only gave two of these permanent places to my part of the RNR. However, the Admiralty Fleet Order did turn up and it said that Lieutenant-Commander Foden was granted a permanent position along with only one of the other chaps, so I thought myself very lucky. The only snag was that if I were to be promoted it would only be an Acting rank, because otherwise officers who had served in the Royal Navy for years would miss out by people like me slipping in.

'I had lunch with Mike Hutton, the Supply Officer from *Bulolo*, who was now Superintending Purser with P & O and was shortly leaving for Australia. He said that he would be able to put me back in straight away, but instead I listened to my mother, who said that this commission would give me some stability. So I decided on this permanent commission.

'It was a great time, with a full and rewarding lifestyle. A note from the Admiralty made me Supply Officer at Coastal Forces Base, *HMS Hornet*, in Gosport. Gillie Potter had just come from there and told me what to watch out for. In early

1954 I was sent to Gosport. However, I took some leave first. That particular Spring was terrible weather, I had snow throughout the trip, all the way back to Bristol. That lovely car, the TC MG was never the same again, the suspension being really ruined by that trip.

'My mother was living alone in Queens court and I felt sorry for her as she was very lonely there. I had kept in touch with a young girl friend from my *Anson* days and I called her and she came up when I was there and persuaded my mother that she should get a paying guest in to keep her company and earn a little money. My mother put an advert in the *Evening Post* and soon a whole host of replies came in. One of them was from Alan Forbes, the Managing Director of Windmill and Lewis (the MG dealer) and later, you guessed it, he married my mother. But first he became a paying guest and helped me a lot with my cars. That leave in Bristol was a very pleasant one. Then I was back on the road and off to Gosport. I returned there with promotion as Supply Officer status.

'Golly what a time. There were lots of young officers looking after Fast Patrol Boats there. It was a super establishment and we really did enjoy ourselves. There was a jolly good Secretary to the Captain at the Station, a chap called Christopher Paul Morgan-Giles, whose brother was the Admiral who later became the MP for Winchester. Christopher and I soon became rivals, buying and selling cars and making a bit of money doing it. He used to specialise in old Bentleys; I used to choose more mundane varieties like the Austin 7s. We were able to use the gunboat yard there for doing up these cars and *Flandern*, my old yacht, had been moved down to Gosport, so we sailed on her once more. I became the local Dinghy Secretary and it was fun but hard work as I was on my own and I had all the returns to do and I wasn't really used to it, so I had to put a lot of time into making sure everything was running smoothly. I had a good Deputy Supply Officer, chap called John Irvin and he was most helpful.

'There used to be a lot of Naval sailing races in Gosport which we could take part in; and also the Royal Ocean Racing Club and their offshoot, the Junior Offshore Club.

'One Saturday we were told that Captain Illingworth was arranging a race for the Junior Offshore Club around the Isle of Wight, quite apart from the annual Round the Island Race. He was arranging this starting from *HMS Hornet* in Gosport. I was the Duty Commanding Officer that weekend and had to make sure everything was operating well for them.

'It was probably blowing about a Force 7 to 8, gusting to Force 9, and I thought that would certainly mean I could push off to the pub. I approached Illingworth feeling sure that the race wouldn't be going ahead and he replied "What bloody rubbish you talk, call yourself a sailor? Get on with it!" So I told my chum who was the Duty Fast Patrol Boat Officer that he had better be quick off the mark when sent out to rescue anyone.

'Illingworth stood his ground and the race went ahead. To my horror, two of the boats were filled with ladies only! Off they all went but almost immediately a de-masted boat needed assistance and it was up to us to rescue the crew as it was really our race. It was one of the lady's crews and the second boat to be rescued was the other lady's crew. I turned in at about 1 o'clock in the morning and by 7 o'clock I thought I had better go and see if the ladies needed anything. I invited them to join me for breakfast and provided amenities for them to dry their clothes.

'The Commander and I were pretty well smitten by three of these ladies and he asked me to invite them out to a pub that evening. The evening came. The Commander had an old

Austin and I had my MG and we had to decide quickly who went in which car. I took one of them and he took two in his car. Actually, we had a jolly nice evening, all together at the pub, and I went on to marry the one to whom I had given a lift in my MG!

*

Chapter 8
Marriage and Malta
April 1955 to December 1958

'My future wife was an ex-WREN and so we spoke the same language. She had a super job in London as a secretary in a branch of Shell which dealt with the bunkering of ships. We became engaged and saw each other at weekends. A normal and very pleasant routine was Sunday church, lunch and then at leisure; on one particular occasion I had to read the lesson. Unfortunately, Daphne couldn't be there that weekend. Afterwards, the Commander let on that I had stolen my fiancée from him, which wasn't true, but he told me I should give her up or marry her! Well, Lt-Comd Christopher Paul Morton-Giles grabbed the diary and the Commander told him to put a date in the diary for our marriage! The first weekend available in October was the 29th, and that was that!

'I was dumbfounded, and the parson immediately stood on his head. I said that it was okay for him, he probably wouldn't be involved in the ceremony as Daphne lived in Worcestershire, in a place called Stoke Bliss, near Bromyard. The Parson said he would travel up after speaking to the local vicar there and sort it out, and so it was that after all those years of taking lots of ladies out and accompanying them, I was to be married, and there was no wriggling out of it! 29th October 1955 was the date. Most of the wardroom of *HMS Hornet* proceeded to watch the event in the Church. I really was terribly in love with this girl.'

Before the wedding day, however:

'We had a stag night at Tenbury Wells, the night before. The Catering Officer offered to provide the wedding cake and was coming up in some van that supplied food to *HMS Hornet*. The chap who owned this van was referred to as the Colonel's Establishment and he certainly provided some excellent supplies to us, specialising in emptying the huge refrigerators in these great liners before their refits and selling the produce to us! Barry Dodds, Lt-Comd, CO of the Motor Torpedo Boat (MTB) Special Services Squadron, was in charge of the catering and he had the Communications Officer with him, driving the van. Luckily, he had taken the precaution of having some mobile telephone or similar device with him and was able to raise the RAC if the van broke down which, inevitably, it did. The cake only just arrived in time and my new in-laws had nearly given up on it.

'We received some dreadful telegrams and lots of awful things were done to Daphne and myself before we went on our honeymoon. We went to a place called the Ferryboat Inn in Helford and managed some pretty idyllic dinghy sailing, even though it was November. It went all too quickly and we returned to our little Coastguard Cottage in Leigh-on-Solent.

'I soon received the letter from the Admiralty that I was expecting. It said I was to go to a NATO job in Malta. I left *HMS Hornet* in April 1956, very sad to do so as I had really enjoyed my time there. I had spent just over two years there and the establishment was ticking like a clock. There was already talk that the Coastal Forces would be closed down for economic reasons and that Gosport would just become a huge Naval Sailing base, and that *HMS Hornet* would just disappear. It all proved correct, of course. All these wonderful things which we had been experimenting with were just thrown out of the window and that was the end of the Coastal Forces.

'John Illingworth, the Engineer Captain of Naval sailing fame was not a bad old chap really; he rather liked Daphne and while I was still with *HMS Hornet*, in the Autumn of 1955, we invited him over for a spot of lunch. I had a 2-seater 1938 Austin 7 down in the gun boat yard which he really wanted off me, so we fixed a price and he took it off my hands. The car didn't last long. He overstepped the mark and turned it over and wrote it off. I was very upset that such a lovely 2-seater car could last for such a short time.'

Tom does remember some very funny stories from these enjoyable days in Gosport:

'As a Bristolian, I was delighted that we had two Bristol Proteus engines in one of the boats, which was called Brave Pathfinder. Basically, it was used for experiments, to see what could be done with it. Well, we made that boat go to unknown speeds for the time, 60 mph was quite considerable! We had to get the boat looking just right and when we thought all was ready invited down lots of chaps from Foreign and Commonwealth Navies, as we saw a possibility to sell these boats. We invited twenty-five in total to come on board and go out in it. We had to pack them in and on the horizon we saw the *Queen Elizabeth*. Someone suggested we go right around her to show how fast we could go. Barry Dodds was driving and we had just got ourselves in position when over our telephone a little voice from the engine room told us that the temperature on the starboard engine was increasing. The Chief said that in another ten minutes he would have to shut the engine down. Well, we knew it would look terrible in front of these people, so we said that we had had a message from the Captain of the *Queen Elizabeth* who had radioed us saying it was too dangerous, so we just kept up to the *Queen Elizabeth's* 30 knots that she was maintaining, right the way up to the Portsmouth entrance, without letting our guests know of our problem. I believe we managed to acquire a few orders as well!

'I must tell you about one of the sailing races before we left Gosport. We had been engaged with the Air Force and the Army in this race and the *Queen Elizabeth* had appeared at that time, too. I suggested to my crew that we should cross her bows, which we attempted, but one long blast from her horn told us to get out of the way! I thought no more of this but next morning the phone rang and the Admiral's Secretary asked me if I was in dinghy number K327. When I told him I was, he said I should go to the Admiral's office with my sword and medals the very next morning, along with the rest of the crew, who I had to name!

'Well, I was very worried by this and when we all arrived at the appointed time the Admiral showed us a signal that he had received from the Captain of the *Queen Elizabeth* asking us very nicely to keep at least a mile between us and them in future. The Admiral was not pleased by our conduct and he made us give up sailing for a month. It was a very nasty shock but he didn't court-martial us!'

So, Daphne and Tom were to leave their cottage in Leigh-on-Solent:

'I was appointed to the NATO Allied Forces in the Mediterranean, based in Malta. I had been to the Admiralty to see what was available and thought that NATO sounded fun as you received a lot of allowances; as I was just married, money was pretty high on my list of requirements. I had a nice lot of leave that Christmas and was then appointed to Malta.

'The first snag was that I was told that my appointment was on 10th April and I would be flying out on 9th! I was not happy with this at all, for I knew it would be some old Viking aircraft flown by an ex-Fleet Air Arm pilot. I was not really that keen, even if they were good pilots. So I went to see the Movements people at the Admiralty and arranged that I could go by sea on a Royal Fleet Auxiliary ship and could use up some of my leave for the trip. So there it was, appointed to the RFA, *Fort Dunvegan*, and my wife and myself and a huge amount of luggage set sail.

'We were passengers along with another ten people as these ships were allowed to carry up to twelve people. We had a charming time. The other passengers included Captain Taprell and Margaret Dorling, an authoress of many Naval books. They both had a great sense of humour and when we got to Gibraltar Captain Taprell played a rather nasty trick on poor Daphne.

'Daphne, as I said, was an ex-WREN and a good communicator, and the Captain of *Fort Dunvegan* got her up on the Bridge sending messages. The Navy could not understand how an RFA was sending such perfect Morse messages so quickly. At dinner that night the Captain asked Daphne if she had heard that some chap was coming with his camels to take her off to a fort in the desert and we would have to go along with this as a lot of blackmail had been done and it would be better if she went off with him since such a huge amount of money had been spent on her behalf. Of course, she went off to bed truly worried and the next day nothing really happened. That night we went to The Rock Hotel for dinner and had a lovely meal. Daphne was a bit more relaxed then. After Gibraltar, we set sail for Malta.'

Malta, of course, brought back its own memories:

'In Malta, when I was in *Bulolo* and we carried out the Anzio Landing, we, of course, took some Italian prisoners. *Bulolo* took about 50 of these on board (one of them gave me his revolver in order to provide him with a nice cabin). I kept that revolver and Daphne was very worried that when we were searched in Malta I would go to prison if it were found. It had to go overboard, along with the ammunition for it. It was really for the best. So we disembarked, tried to find some accommodation and were put in the Astra Hotel in Sliema, while we found something more suitable. Very fortunately, when I had been in Malta in *Breconshire* I knew an old Maltese Colonel, Etti Borge, and so I went straight away to see him. Funnily enough, the hotel in which we were staying was owned by him and we were invited to stay as long as we wanted to. He also said that he had a first-floor flat in his compound, near to his beautiful house in Birkikara Street, Sliema, and we could have this flat as someone had just left it. We moved into this flat for a fair rent and ended up staying there for the whole of that commission. I think that some of the guys in the Headquarters Allied Forces Mediterranean were a little envious we had found accommodation so easily.

'We had a jolly nice French Navy Captain living near us, a chap called Favre. He was married to an English girl who had been a barmaid in the West End; he had been in the Free French Navy when they met. They had a beautiful dog, a chow called Chow, and they were truly a charming couple.'

Inevitably, once accommodation had been found, Tom would require a car:

'I knew that the next thing to do was to get a motor car. With NATO you didn't pay duty on a car, which made them incredibly cheap. I thought a Fiat 600 would be small and convenient and just right for Malta. Meanwhile, I found out that the guy who ran the Fiat agency was Major Henny Scicluna, who had been in charge of the Bofors Guns that had protected the *Breconshire* while she had been in Marsaslokk Bay. It was very nice to see him again and he went out of his way to find me this lovely little Fiat, which he took the trouble to look after while we stayed in Malta.'

Tom tells us a little about his work:

'My job involved looking after the Annual Financial Estimates and getting the money from NATO for a Forward

Scatter System for the Communications in Malta. My boss was a civilian, Jeffrey Moses who was a Principal Under Secretary in the Ministry of Defence. We went all around the Mediterranean together. There was also a British Admiral, Admiral Robertshaw, whom I had come across in my *Bulolo* days. He had been the Chief-of-Staff for Force G which was our Force for the Normandy landings. He had granted the G licence for me so that I could get all the petrol that I required in those days. We knew each other quite well and Robertshaw was also pretty keen on sailing. Luckily, the Naval Yacht, the *Flandern,* had found its way out to Malta and so we were fairly well set up for some decent sailing. I also requested funds for buying a couple of dinghies and we all belonged to the Royal Malta Yacht Club, and there were also Royal Naval Sailing Association facilities there which we could use.

'By now, of course, there were all sorts of people in NATO, Greeks, Turks, Italians, French Canadians and Americans, as well as ourselves. The Germans were just coming in. One of the earliest events that I remember was that we had a party of German Officers coming to stay with us. They hadn't actually signed on for NATO and we were pushing them like mad to do so. The Admiral asked Daphne and myself to entertain these chaps. Luckily, Daphne could speak a little German and they were ushered into the bar at HAFMED when they arrived. I started talking to one chap who asked me which ship I had been in and I told him the unfortunate happenings of *Salopian.* Call it coincidence, this chap was the First Lieutenant on the German submarine that had sunk us!

'Instead of being dreadful enemies, we became real friends. He told me that the Captain was a very Holy Man and was incredibly sad when he had been forced to sink *Salopian.* The German captain knew what he had to do but he had been hopping mad with our Captain. We stayed friends and exchanged Christmas cards for many years after that meeting. We did a lot of good work in Malta, especially towards the Germans and we persuaded them that NATO was doing a fine job out there. It was hard work though. We went on slowly building up the NATO Forces. It was still very early days.'

Tom met many people on Malta whom he had seen before:

'Mr Mifsud, the big travel Agent in Malta, who, again, I had come across in my *Breconshire* days, was another of these. He was very good to us with our travel arrangements, not only to me, but for the whole of the NATO HQ Mediterranean. He gave us a decent discount which helped us along. But as I say, on my own personal front, he was particularly helpful with the little trips we took with Captain Tuleio Angheben in *Citta de Benghazi.*'

One event in particular remains clear in Tom's mind:

'As I said, Mr Mifsud was good to us and set us up on passages with Captain Tuleio Angheben who was very good to my wife and me. He had been a Gunnery Officer in the *Vittoria.* This was the Italian battleship, when I was on the *Breconshire* and as I said, we never took a direct hit from them! However, it was peacetime now and he was captain of this lovely little passenger ship, on which we used to take trips to Benghazi. We were able to go for a few days and really enjoyed ourselves. We got to know him quite well as I was a passenger with him on many occasions, right from the first trip to Naples where I went to a NATO Conference in 1957.

'When we went to Benghazi, the Captain said we should take our car. So we took the Fiat, and the policemen wished us well. Tourism was just beginning to start up in North Africa so we were made very welcome indeed. There we stayed for a few lovely days and then went back and settled down to normal life after this three day trip.

'A few days later, I was looking out of my window over the Grand Harbour when the *Citta de Benghazi* was disembarking her passengers. I watched while they did all of this. They embarked new passengers and the time came to take up the anchor, which they started to do: and there, lo and behold, a mine was sitting quietly on the fluke! The passengers and crew either rushed down the gangway or over the side, leaving the Captain and the Chief Officer on board.

'Well, Captain Tuleio Angheben showed his real strength. He locked the door to the engine room so none of them could get out and then called them up to let them know what had happened. He said that they would be going astern fairly shortly, and that was exactly what they did. He called the Port Control and asked for instructions. They told him to go astern very carefully and leave the Grand Harbour, and meanwhile the port Authorities would do everything they could to keep the harbour empty. All the Emergency Services stood by and I realised that something was going on. We were told to go to the basement shelter.

'Well, the Captain left the harbour and let the mine go and returned to his moorings. In a day or two, the RN blew the mine up and we all realised how lucky we had been. Meanwhile, Admiral Robertshaw and his secretary, Teddy Astley-Jones acknowledged that the Captain should be recognised for his bravery. Teddy suggested that we put him up for a British decoration, which meant more to these chaps anyway. It was decided that an OBE would be appropriate, the Queen acknowledged this and in due course Admiral Cunningham, who was also the Governor General of Malta, decorated him. He was now Captain, Count Tuleio Angheben OBE, and was probably unique in this situation. But he really did deserve it. I shall never forget his bravery. Soon after this, his shipping line realised that they had a great Captain and he was promoted to the *Citta de Napoli*, which was on the same service but was a beautiful brand-new ship. We were very lucky to be able to go one weekend to Sicily with him on this ship. We landed in Syracuse, taking the car with us on that trip as well. We found it a very lovely island, happily staying in a super hotel right up in the hills about forty miles from Syracuse.'

Tom reminds us that these times were short-lived:

'Sadly, our days were coming to a close. We had a very happy two years there and we had built up NATO, as I said before. The Maltese Government had always been against us. Don Mintoff had taken over as Prime Minister and it was still a British Colony, which gave him rather a lot of problems. He was not sure whether that was the right way to go, but we had him to dinner one evening. He had a very sensible English wife. He was not anti-British at all but what he wanted was for the British Government to actually take on Malta in a similar sort of scheme that already operated in the Channel Islands. However, Britain could not afford to do that; operating the Health Service, alone, would have incurred immense costs. The British, therefore, told him that they would be delighted to have Malta as part of the Commonwealth but could not give them all the money that he required. Mintoff was not interested in half measures and thought he would approach the North African countries instead. He did, went to Tripoli and approached Colonel Gaddafi. The Maltese people realised that this would be a real tragedy, but they could not stop Mintoff in his plan. After Mintoff, the next chap unscrambled this problem but the damage had been done and Malta was never very close to Britain again.

'The Dockyard, which had been the envy of the whole Mediterranean, was sold to CJ Bailey of South Wales, who thought they would be able to do what they liked with it,

117

which, of course, was not correct. There were plenty of strikes from the workforce, the Welsh company then sold the dockyard on to the Russians and the area declined completely, along with the rest of the Maltese economy. They only had themselves to thank for this, which was a very, very sad event.'

Tom had first-hand experience of the Royal Naval Hospital at Bighi before he left Malta:

'I was recovering from a varicose vein operation to my other leg when the Senior Nursing Sister for the area of the hospital I was in told me of the goings-on of the week earlier. Apparently, a very senior Naval officer had been in the hospital for routine surgery; but he was not one of the most popular patients and the male Sick Berth Attendants were determined to cause some slight Hoo-Ha. Among them was a very clever make-up artist in civil life who had made one of his colleagues look anything other than his normal self! This man took the Senior Officer's temperature at the usual time in the evening and pronounced his great concern at its reading. After taking it again, he inferred that it was still high. The SBA asked the patient to turn over and allow his temperature to be taken with the thermometer in his bottom. Once this was organised the SBA went out of the room to fetch the Duty Medical Officer. You must understand, this was all beautifully engineered for the arrival of Senior Matron, who joined this Senior Naval Officer for a gin at about that time. Well, of course, she arrived to see a rose protruding from the said gentleman's bottom and she expressed her great surprise and concern! The perpetrator was never discovered but the tale went around the hospital and most of Malta. The Senior Naval Officer never lived it down. Some say this incident became the inspiration for a scene in one of the 'Carry On' films with Hattie Jacques as the Matron.'

Tom and Daphne were coming to the end of their time in Malta:

'I had to think about making my own move now. My two years were up and I was being relieved in the September of 1958. I didn't know by whom, though. Admiral Robertshaw, who had been such a good support, had also been relieved, along with Admiral Perrigini, the Italian Admiral. The American Admiral, who had taken over as C-in-C, Admiral Cato D. Glover, had also been relieved and Suez was going on by then, so it was a good thing everyone went together, really. We had lots of parties to say goodbye to everyone.

'I had carefully planned my voyage back to the UK in our little Fiat 600. Naturally, I had arranged it with Captain Angheben and when the *Citta de Napoli* was in harbour we availed ourselves of his facilities. It came to the sad time when we went down to the Grand Harbour, lifted the Fiat on board with our possessions and off we went. We had a super voyage.

'The day before we arrived in Naples, we had a lovely farewell party. In an Italian ship, they are rather better found than our ships of similar status. There was the Captain, Chief, First, Second and Third Officers and also the Purser and Chief Engineer, and it was decided that the Captain could have a few drinks with us and leave the ship to the Chief Officer until he wished to take over.

'The way the Italians run these ships is far better than people think. They were smart, ran the ship well, especially in an emergency, which gave complete confidence, and had excellent cooks on board, too. Unfortunately, the *Andrea Doria* incident was a lapse that made news, but they seem to improve all the time, just getting better and better. They come to the Royal Portbury Docks, here in Bristol now and they are some of the smartest ships there.'

Tom continues with the voyage:

'Anyway, we stayed in various Italian ports all the way up, until we left the border for France. The Fiat distributor from Malta, I mentioned him earlier, Henny Scicluna, arranged for our Fiat to go into the Fiat facility at Naples for a full service. We went to a lovely fish restaurant down on the quay that evening in Naples and the next day, having a bit of trouble finding the Fiat place, we arrived a few minutes late. A Count, a real gentleman in Saville Row suiting, immaculately dressed, came to meet me, and after he greeted me mentioned that it was not usual for a Commander of the RN to be ten minutes late! He then arranged for the car to be taken by someone to be serviced before we started on our voyage to the UK. He took us to his quarters just outside the workplace and we had a lovely luncheon and siesta there, and then our car turned up and we went on back, slowly, due to the traffic in Naples, to our hotel. We sent him some flowers and he wrote a lovely note which was waiting for us in England when we arrived back! Fiat had not made any charge for the work that they carried out for us.'

Tom talks of the trip back on land:

'We had a super run up through Italy, the hotels in all the Naval bases were terrific, beautifully run, and at each place, we were very well received by the Captain of the port and given clearance. France was a little different, for we were away from the sea now. We travelled on until we got to Cherbourg and managed to catch the Silver City Aircraft with an hour to spare. We got in this lovely Bristol-made aircraft; I have never been in an aircraft which vibrated so much but the crew didn't seem to take any notice. We landed on a grass runway at Southampton where my mother met us and we went to the Paragon Hotel in Southampton for our first night back in the UK.'

*

Chapter 9
Northwood, Haslemere
December 1958 to September 1962

'It was a bit of a shock coming back. The England that I had known was now more advanced in that two years than I had seen on returning home before. There were motorways springing up all over the place and very few signs of the war about.'

Tom and Daphne settled quickly:

'I managed to rent a house from a fellow NATO chum who was leaving for £40 a week. It was just outside Chichester and had a lovely swimming pool. We couldn't really afford it, but it was such a lovely place. At the same time, I bought Daphne a little car as well. After a few weeks, I was requested to attend the Admiralty and find out where I was going next. I thought that I might be sent to Haslemere, which was fine, except for the chap in charge. The Commanding Officer there was not a very popular man. However, the Admiralty told me that they were very short-handed and they would not allow me all the leave to which I was entitled after two years away and I was to go up to Northwood where the Admiralty were making a hole in the ground for the Nuclear HQ of the Home Fleet and the local NATO Command.

'My job was to study the plans and with two other Officers, FAA and RAF chaps, to decide on the equipment that was necessary to make this new HQ a fine, upstanding and well-run establishment. I did not think that this was fair, as I had no idea what was going to be involved, or the support that I would get. However, there was little choice and I was to report in at RAF Northwood. The Admiralty assured me that I would get full support, I would be a member of the Mess and I would have my quarters at Northwood House, soon to be the C-in-C's house. I felt very happy after all these reassurances.

'Sadly, there was nothing in the galley of this house, so we went and got ourselves a Baby Belling cooker. Well, the buzz got around that the Fodens could prepare some very good meals at Northwood House so we ended up with lots of friends. We cooked for twenty-two one night! I was also studying the notice board in the Station for any likely bargains. Sure enough, I saw a Douglas motorcycle for sale, a 1951 model, so it was not very old. The owner was required for duty and needed to sell his bike quickly. I went and had a look at it, rode it around the driveways on the Base and then took it on the road. He wanted £30 and I offered £25, which was quite enough for it, and he accepted. My wife was horrified and didn't want me to ride it. However, I did! I used to ride it about a mile and a half to the Base, without a licence. Within a very short period of time, I started a new lease of life on this bike and eventually taxed and insured it, as well!'

The three chaps were trying to sort out what was needed at HQ:

'We three did our best to stock this Headquarters and thoroughly enjoyed the work. The Admiralty didn't give us a great amount of time to sort this all out. By March 1959 they wanted me to go to the staff of the Commodore Naval Drafting at Haslemere, so we had to have the removal people in to come and take our furniture, which we had brought back from Malta, out of Northwood, down to Midhurst. I realise that I had been very lucky with my quarters and that things would not be the same at Haslemere, because although they give you a generous allowance to compensate, they did not have any quarters there.

'Anyway, a chum of mine told me about a house at Esborne, near Midhurst where an old lady had a property known as

'Highmead.' She rented the place out, if she liked the look of the prospective tenant, because she ran a charity in London most of the time. The only thing that I had to do was make sure that there would always be a room kept for her. We weren't terribly happy with this, but we decided to go along with it. It was a five-bedroomed house with a huge garden and a large garage. Daphne made full use of the vegetable garden and I mowed the lawns with a push mower, no sit-on mower there!

'We settled in nicely, relaxing for a week before I started my new job. I was in a little bit of trepidation as one of my previous officers thought that I should go in *HMS Protector* to the Falklands, or something. Anyway, I liked the idea of being in the country. Well, when I met up with the Commander, I was told the Commodore would see me at 10 o'clock and it was then that I realised what it was the officer was trying to tell me. This Commodore was similar to going back to Nelson's time and he made it clear that he did not suffer fools gladly. I informed him that I already knew a Captain Kershaw, in person, who had always said that to me. He replied that I probably couldn't stand up to the pace!

'The very next day, we all had lunch in a nice anteroom, which was separated from the lovely Lyehill House (which was the HQ for the appointing of sailors, where I dealt with the Supply Ratings). Anyhow, we went into lunch and the Commodore was there. I was talking a bit of shop to a chum when the Commodore told us to shut up. It was obvious that I was not going to get an easy ride with him. I was determined to go to him in the afternoon and suggest that he got someone more suited to the job but his Secretary advised me to leave the Commodore alone, and so I did.

'It wasn't long before another chum of mine, from *HMS Anson*, Joseph Bartisik, charming officer with a lovely WREN wife, fetched up. When I was working in *Anson* he was a Lt-Comd and I was a very junior one. He was now Captain of the Fifth Frigate Squadron and wanted a really good group of Writers, Stores assistants, Cooks and Stewards for his senior ship. It was quite late in the day and I was on my own, so I was delighted to help him; I got hold of the records of the ratings who were available and we seemed to have done rather well with some good chaps. That evening, I suggested that he come and stay with Daphne and me and we would all have supper together. The Commodore buzzed me on the intercom at that moment and reminded me that it was usual for officers to report to him when they came to visit this establishment. Bartisik had to explain to the Commodore why he was there and the Commodore made it quite clear that he was the person who was Boss. Anyway, the Commodore wanted to know who I had suggested and when he saw the list had a few ideas of his own. He asked to be brought the complete list and picked out the worst ones he could find and gave him just the worst person he could to be his Steward.

'This chap had been Admiral Myer's Steward in Cyprus, but had blotted his copy book: one night he got hold of an alarm clock and set it to go off at 3 o'clock in the morning when everyone was asleep - until they heard this damn clock ringing. Most of them rushed around to see what was ringing and found it, but not the culprit. A few days later when a visiting American Squadron was there this Steward swapped the brandy and ginger-ale bottles around and created a lot of chaos. When it became clear what had happened the Admiral had had enough: the man was sent to Preston Detention Quarters for thirty days penance. Now, the Commodore was offering him to Bartisik!

'Well, the Commodore was a bit taken aback by Bartisik's forthright attitude and off we went to a very late supper at home. About a year later we went aboard Bartisik's ship and met the chap; he had turned out to be an excellent Steward and actually came up to thank me for giving him such a wonderful chance. A few years after that he turned up as the Catering Officer on board a ship I was visiting: he certainly became one of the best Catering Officer's the Navy has ever had. It had all rather backfired on the Commodore.

'I thought that with the Commodore's attitude as it was, there was every chance that I would be court-martialled over something or other, but in fact he mellowed a little bit. Then it was only a waiting game till he retired, himself. Before then, however, there was an event regarding a telephone.

'One morning someone at the Portsmouth Naval Exchange made me hopping mad, and he and I exchanged a few heated words. It wasn't long before the Commodore hauled me in and said that the supervisor there, a lovely lass, had called him and said that I was extremely rude, arrogant and very unhelpful to one of her lads that morning. I explained to the Commodore, but of course he did not really believe that the chap had been rude and unhelpful to me and had not given me the information I required. The Commodore replied that I must have been as rude and tactless as can be and that that would reflect on the Establishment and the Flag Officer, Portsmouth. He then informed me that our Administrative Authority would get to hear about it and would be very displeased, and that it would have to be reported on my documents. He turned away from me and seemed to be ignoring me. And then he said "Forget it, that's the very last time you will get away with it!" He told me I was too clever for the Navy and I should get out of his sight. He didn't leave very long after that himself.'

Before his departure, Tom remembers:

'I had a Triumph Herald Coupe as well as the bike and the Commodore bought a new Herald Saloon. He actually liked this car and would show it off to the other officers whenever he could, and in the final months before he went, we got on jolly well. After that, we had the most charming Commodore that I have ever had the fortune to serve with, he was an absolutely poised Naval Officer, approachable and helpful, Raymond Hart was his name. He had been very mixed up in the Battle of the Atlantic, had a great fighting history and was a great seaman. He was ex-RNR and had spent time with the Royal Mail Lines until he got his commission in the Royal Navy. He knew he would not be promoted to Admiral, it was part of the understanding when he was commissioned, just as mine was. He had married a lovely lady, Peggy, and they had an attractive old house, called Tree Firs, Bramshot Chase, Hindhead. They had wonderful dances there, very lavish and exciting, but in a funny way Ray did not have any time for anyone who didn't pull their weight. To one of these dances in particular, held in December 1961, I had invited a chum along from the Admiralty to see if I could find out what my next job might be. You see, I was open to offers.'

*

Tom and his chums on one of *Bulolo's* Landing Craft. In the background is the residential complex owned by Martin Lee's family, Singapore.

The MG buried in Singapore and then dug up after the departure of the Japanese.

Captain C A Kershaw RN, Captain of the Flagship *HMS Bulolo*.

Captain R.L. Hamer RN, Captain of *HMS Bulolo*, with his Commander.

Daphne, Tom's first wife, on board their yacht, *Truelove*, close to their mooring in Malta Bay.

HIH Rear Admiral Alexander Desta with Captain Peter Stewart IEN, Commander Naval Base, Masawa.

His Imperial Highness Haile Selassie I bestowing a Diploma on Dr Araya Redda in Addis Ababa in 1974. At a similar Ceremony Tom was awarded a gold tie clip.

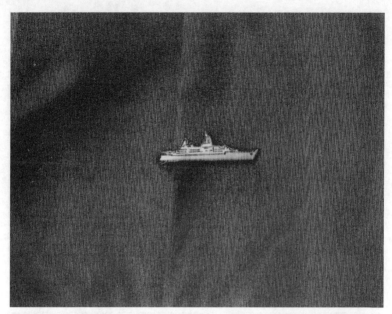

The gold tie clip fashioned as *HIMS Ethiopia*, presented to Tom by HIH Haile Selassie I.

Commander and Mrs Tom Foden being presented to HM Queen Elizabeth II during her visit to Bristol on 8 August 1977.

Paddle Steamer Waverley.

Motor Vessel Balmoral.

Chapter 10
The Ghana Navy
September 1962 to July 1966

Tom really was in a dilemma! The chap who turned up to the dance informed him that the Admiralty wanted someone to be the Deputy Head of the Trinidad Navy, which was just starting up. Tom continues:

'Well, I said it sounded right up my street and with a few courses bringing me up to date on procedures it seemed that I would be able to do the job. So, it was all set up and I started to pack up my job and my wife and the house in Midhurst. This chum then gave me a call and told me that they couldn't send me because Trinidad couldn't afford to have a Naval Commander as Deputy; they were going to choose a much more junior person! However, there seemed to be a similar job going in Ghana. I could not picture where this was and when he told me it was in West Africa, I knew then that it was formerly called The Gold Coast. I had passed it a couple of times when I was *on HMS Bulolo*. Daphne and I looked at the maps, had a chat with someone who knew the place and we made our minds up that we would give it a go. "Get on with it", so to speak.'

I am sure that it all becomes a lot clearer when you hear the background to the whole Ghana package.

'We had a few advantages there in the British Joint Services Training Team: a duty-free car and duty-free spirits were amongst them. We gave a party when we left Haslemere feeling a bit sad, for it had been a happy time there, especially under Commodore Raymond Hart. We sold all my cars: a lovely Austin 7 sports (to my secretary) and a Fiat. I looked forward to a new car, duty-free, which I was taking to Ghana; another Fiat, a 600, top of the range, very compact and very reliable.

'The Naval Authorities wrote to me to let me know that I had been appointed to Ghana and that I would be travelling by Ghana Airways on such and such a date. Well, I was not at all happy about this and called them up and asked if I could go by sea. I knew about the *Auriol*, the flagship of the Elder Dempster Line which plied between the UK and Ghana, and I was quite happy for the time that the trip would take to come off my leave allowance. Well, they looked into it and found nothing wrong with my request and so we travelled by ship instead. We were leaving from Liverpool and joined the *Auriol* there, saying our goodbyes to my mother and her third husband, who came to see us off.

'It was a tremendously interesting voyage for us both, and we met a great variety of people on board: one of the judges who was going to work on the Western circuit in Nigeria and a Nigerian who was the Director of the Prisons there. We had a lovely trip, stopping in Las Palmas for some tropical wear and other goodies. I was surprised to see so many Russian trawlers in the port there but the Captain told me that they were really re-fuelling their submarines. I asked him if they were reporting the Russian's activities and he said he was generally keeping an eye on it all!

'On arrival in Ghana Commander John Murray met us in his car and took us to Burma Camp, the Headquarters of the Ghana Navy, where I met up with the Commodore. He was, obviously, a black man, an absolutely charming chap called David Hansom, and everything looked okay. The climate was quite pleasant, not unduly hot or humid.

'Our quarters were not ready because the chap I was replacing was waiting for the *Auriol* to finish her trip around the West Coast before returning to pick him, and other passengers, up and then head back to the UK. Meanwhile, we went into some transit quarters which were fine and comfortable. The only snag was that we had not been there for more than a few days when we were told the Nigerians were sending a submarine to attack the President! Anyway, we had to go to 'Action Stations'. It all seemed to be a bit far fetched, but the only thing that I got was a bad tummy from eating something in haste during this time. My wife also had a stomach upset but apart from that we were okay with the quarters that we had. Every day I wished that my car had come, as I was given some old wreck to use that had to be cranked or pushed every time you started it. I wasn't keen to drive it anywhere off camp.'

Tom continues:

'Well, by the time the car turned up I had taken up my position as Second Senior Officer, in line with the Fleet Engineer Officer and another Commander who were both Royal Navy. All the senior officers were RN.

'The President, Nkrumah, was a great chap. The Nigerians were considering buying an aircraft carrier and it was well known that the Ghana Navy would want one, too. I had to be fairly circumspect with him as I knew that Ghana couldn't afford one. Also, it would have meant a lot of white staff on board, which would have been embarrassing when visiting black African ports. The President quietly said he would deal with the finance and that the Ghana Commercial Stores had plenty of Cherry Blossom black boot polish for the white faces! The whole idea was dropped.'

Tom explains the political situation:

'Ghana is now a junior member of the Senior Common-wealth Countries, promoted by the Queen on a visit in AD 2000. One of the Ghana Bishops, a Naval Chaplain in my day, came to stay with us recently. He said what a super little country it was now; they had no money, just got on with everything themselves and were going from strength to strength. There seemed to be an upward curve taking them beyond their troubles.'

Tom explains his early days there:

'There was always something going wrong or having to be done when I was there! It was enjoyable, though, and there was lots of socialising between the Services and the Diplomatic Corps.

'My wife started a sewing class; the Russian boss's wife was very young and attractive and wanted to join these classes. I mentioned this to the High Commissioner and he refused that option totally. I had the excuse that the classes were only for the English!

'The President wanted some patrol boats at about this time. The Russians were going to make a couple available to him. We had a young Ghanaian Midshipman, Blekpe, who had just returned from a course in Russia and was my assistant. He realised they were going to get these fast boats from the Russians and asked me to have a look at them: when we had talked in confidence he had told me that they were old, from around 1914/15, and had just been polished up. He said they would cause us nothing but trouble, so I told the Admiral, who said we would have to go ahead with the patrol boats because the Russian Ambassador had persuaded the President to have them.

'Well, it was very interesting. A charming Lieutenant-Commander, the Russian Naval Attache, came to see me and told me he had a terrible problem as these two patrol boats had arrived and when he had looked at them the paint had come off them as they were designed only for freshwater use. Well, he wanted me to sell him some RN grey paint to cover up the evidence of the terrible paint work. I would not do it!

'I told him that I would ask the Admiralty about this and he said that that would be most helpful. I sent a confidential message to the High Commissioner and the Commissioner asked me to send a signal to the Admiralty and he was going to send one to the Foreign Office as well, as he was not sure but felt that they might ask us to carry out the work. He was not sure if this young Russian Officer might well defect. Well, the approval arrived and was paid up without blinking an eyelid. The Stores Officer couldn't believe it either and the boats were soon painted up. The Russian was the hero of the moment. He really wanted them to be top class and suggested that they try them out on trials before the great day of handing them over. Well, the day came and we were there with the President aboard his yacht, *Ashimota*. Champagne and sparkling wine were delivered to all.

'Blekpe said he would come and have a meal with me the following Tuesday with his wife. We had a pleasant evening, parting on good terms. Anyway, we had terrible trouble with these boats and kept them in reserve. A few months later I was speaking to the Russian Ambassador at a party. Well, I asked about the Russian officer and was told he had gone back to Russia!'

Tom enlarges:

'I had my spies. Mostly the young black Midshipman again, who knew people at the Russian Embassy. (He was just as good as an RN Midshipman.) Anyway, he told us what had happened. The chap had been ordered back to Moscow because he was too interested in us. He knew well enough that he would be in trouble when he arrived there so he and his wife went to the American Embassy when they reached Egypt and asked for asylum, then were sent to the USA to be de-briefed.

'Another incident was when some general from Russia was due to come to visit us. No-one told him it was warm in Ghana and there he was, poor chap, in full dress uniform. But that was the sort of thing that went on. They were good but not as good as the Press led us to believe. They had a lot to learn!

'About this time an American colonel, Ralph Williams, a black man with an equally charming black wife, Velma, took up the job of Defence Attache, We became very friendly with them. One night he said he had news for us: in about six weeks time we were to receive a new Ambassador, Shirley Temple-Black. She arrived and settled in well. When any party got out of hand, people would start singing "On the good ship lollipop." She sang it for us on one occasion, but anyway, hearing it made things a lot easier. When I first went to Ghana things were a little fraught, everyone was trying not to make mistakes and therefore was stressed.

'Sadly, the time came when the President had to go. The Army just couldn't put up with what was going on with the Chinese. All the Armed Forces at the top level had been trained in England and just couldn't put up with it, not at all. A lot of people said I would know that there was a mutiny going on when it happened, but I didn't know at all. Anyhow, when the President went off to China to see their President it was just too much. They went in and toppled him.

'I was unaware that the coup was going to happen. Brigadier Grismond Davies-Scourfield was in charge of the British training team, of which I was the second-senior RN member and I'm pretty certain that the brigadier didn't know what was going on, either.

'Sadly, my house was in the firing line, being situated between State House, where the President lived, and Burma

Camp, where the quarters were, so our roof was peppered with bullets. There was a lot of damage to my furniture from the rain which subsequently came in. The next day there was a terrific storm and the rain caused even more damage.

'Well, we were woken up one morning to the sound of gunfire and as we had arranged for such times I went up to see if the Admiral was all right. He was very concerned, and told me that there was a coup to topple the President.

'As is usual for the Navy, we had to sail all the ships out of port so that they could not take part in the events that followed. There was only the HQ staff left, and the staff at Naval Base at Takoradi. We just sat through the day, it was awful. It wasn't safe to go out, so we stayed in our quarters as some of the soldiers were a little trigger happy. Very fortunately, the Elder Dempster liner was there at the time and we stopped her sailing, just in case we needed her to get some of the Brits away.

'Lots of nasty Russian aeroplanes were coming towards us, or so we were led to understand from the radar, but the "over-flight" turned out to be birds, several hundreds of them actually! So we just sat back and I told my wife that things were not looking good.'

Tom tells us of the situation at that time:

'The sad thoughts I had then were for the Chinese. They, of course, had a lot of influence in Ghana then and had a regiment to protect the President. Unfortunately, the President did not trust his own Army, so when this coup started the Chinese went to look after the State House. The President was no longer there and these Chinese chaps went into a bunker under the house and an officer in the Ghanaian Regiment had to deal with them. He had been promoted and was now Brigadier Kotoka and he informed them that they had to come out and surrender or he would have to take dire measures. As the day went on, he became more and more fed up with them and threatened them with having the bunker sealed up. He was going to get some bricklayers to come and brick it up. Unfortunately, that is exactly what happened. They wouldn't come out and they were very stupid and they had been given every opportunity but they just didn't take it.'

Terrible times indeed:

'Along with such terrible atrocities, when the President went off to Egypt from China we were left to deal with the President's ex-WREN secretary and have her repatriated, along with a British chap called Bing who was Aide to the President. We made sure that these people left the Country. We saw a lot of Bing's secretary, an ex WREN officer, who stayed on for a while, but the new President, General Ankrah, asked her to go as he feared for her safety. After this sort of thing, everyone thinks a country will come out of the doldrums and things will be different, but things did not really change very quickly.

'General Ankrah was a charming old boy. I would pop up there with papers about 10 o'clock in the morning. The Army were self-sufficient but I would go with my Ghanaian opposite number in the Ghana Armed Forces and the General would ask me what I had for him. He used to say that he was just a West African sergeant, really, and if I thought these documents were okay to sign, then he would sign them! So I used to spend half the night checking the documents and let him know if they were okay the next morning. I think that anyone would have done the same; he trusted me and I very much appreciated that and was very careful about what he signed. He had a nice family, too, and we had a lot of fun together.

'There was also the Chief of the General Staff, the general in command of all the Armed Forces, General Stephen Otu. He was a very nice gentleman, too, and had been one of very few African officers in the Royal West African Frontier Force, so he had been at the job for a very long time. He spoke perfect English and used to be very keen on fish.

'I had a 'folk-boat' built in Ghana by the Ghanaian Ship builders at Tema. Daphne and I used to go out every Sunday after Church and one of our dodges was that we would take a little bit of change and when we got over the horizon would go up to some of the fishing boats and barter for some fish. They thought it was great, as it was a bit of pocket money for them. It cost about £2 for a week's supply. We used to go home via the General's house and have a couple of brandy and ginger-ales before going off home. We were very sorry when he left; it was a little political and he used to get on very well with Nkrumah and the powers thought it would be better if there was not so much familiarity.

'General Ankrah was now the President, which was a very good move. He was the C-in-C as well and had General Kotoka as his Second-in-Command, so we had good chaps at the top, pro-British, as Ghana is today. The Queen's visit in the Spring of 2000 was very well received, and the Country was promoted in the Commonwealth.'

After the coup, Tom shows us how life settled down a little:

'Life was quiet. The Navy had reached a superb level of efficiency. The main worry was from the Nigerians, and most of our work was involved in stopping the smuggling racket. Our little ships patrolled the Coast and we made some great catches! We used to bring these back to Tema, using a couple of Army trucks and filling them with drink, cigarettes, perfume and other sundries that we had confiscated. Of course, I asked the General what we were to do about all this contraband. Well, what we actually did with it was to share it with the Armed Forces messes, throughout the Country! So we were never short of goodies. We just used to work harder when we were running a bit short again!

'Those smugglers were not fools. They had machine guns on board and they used canoes with outboards on the back of them; they really moved. Our new Corvettes, the *Keta* and *Kromantse*, built in the UK, were pretty nippy but we could only just hold our own against these canoes. We were required to issue smugglers with a command to stop and if they refused three times we were obliged to fire a shell across their bows. Unfortunately, they would return this with machine-gun fire until they came to their senses and handed over the smuggled goods. The canoes could just run up on the beach as well, a manoeuvre which we were unable to carry out.

'Along with the machine guns on the canoes, the smugglers had guns ashore where they landed, so it was pretty hairy sometimes. At a cocktail party sometimes a high ranking officer would tell me I was being too harsh on the smugglers and could I let off for a while; that usually meant that he probably had some financial interest in the enterprise.

'We had a dear old, retired British Customs Officer there, about 70 or 80 years of age. He knew all the dodges of the game.

'Now and then the President held a big International Conference and used to send one of us chaps to Gibraltar in his big yacht armed with a fistful of Travellers Cheques to go to Saccone and Speed, the drinks dealer there. We had strict instructions to buy up lots of drink and fill up the yacht, which returned filled literally down to the Plimsoll Line with drink.

'The problem was to unload the drink and cigarettes without the Customs Officers being aware. We could have just said it was for official use but it would have created a bad precedent in the Customs people's eyes. So the General informed the old British Customs Officer that he wanted all of his officers to spend a couple of days in the Upper Volta Region to sort out the dreadful smuggling that was going on there. This would, of course, coincide with the return of *Ashimota*, the President's yacht. Terrible really! However, we knew that the Customs guys were actually a damn fine bunch as we never had a drugs problem.'

Tom explains how the politics were around the end of the Nkrumah regime:

'In the latter days of Nkrumah, we had an organisation that was supposed to be planning the invasion of South Africa by other parts of Africa. In this little enclave there was a lovely Egyptian officer.

'They were a nice group of people but they occasionally over-stepped the mark by producing a paper on how they were going to invade South Africa! Sadly, the time came when the Ghana Navy had to be inspected by an RN Admiral from the UK. We just could not find one, so instead of an RN Admiral we were told that we were getting the RN South Atlantic Commander-in-Chief, based at Simonstown, South Africa, to do the job. I couldn't believe it. I told Admiral David Henson but he wasn't worried so long as the chap brought some oranges up with him. However, I let the President's WREN know. No-one seemed worried about it at all, except me.

'Anyway, the Inspecting Officer came up and we got a good report from him after the inspection. His last job was to inspect the people planning the invasion of South Africa; he even gave them some advice on where to invade and suggested that they quietly forget about it. The organisation eventually fizzled out but it was hanging over our heads for quite a while.'

Tom talks of the Navy Personnel:

'One of my best Officers was Lt-Cdr Monty Provencal, a lovely Ghanaian who, sadly, died in 1998. 'Monty' came to see me about a rather touchy subject one day. He said that he and a chum of his had heard that one of the Ghana Black Star Line ships was taking a cargo to Cape Town and he wanted to go with them. I couldn't believe it, but he said he wanted to go and have a look at the place. He had heard that it was a damn good place and he wanted to increase his professional knowledge - and he had heard that the girls weren't bad either! Well, I suggested that some papers needed to be made up and if anything should happen to him then it wasn't the Ghana Navy's fault. He did go and I was very apprehensive but he was fine, and when he returned said that it was a great place. He had tried to make a nuisance of himself, even going into white night clubs, and in uniform as well, but he said that the people were all jolly nice and he could not find any trouble there at all.

'The Press got wind of this little trip that Monty had made and they also said that the people were very friendly when they had been there, too. So it seemed that South Africa was no trouble at all. The South Africans must have been very clever in their dealings with foreigners but it did open my eyes a bit. Monty later joined the Black Star Line from the Ghana Navy. He came into Avonmouth on a few occasions and visited me here, at Clevedon. He used to come and say a few words of wisdom in our little church here when he visited. He was a really nice chap. I was very sad when he died. He had a heart attack when the ship was at sea and they did not have any medical attention on board that was good enough to save him. He was the sort of guy that was a credit to Ghana, one of the best countries in black Africa.'

Tom's interests in cars continued in Ghana:

'I was rather interested in motor cars and sailing, as you well know. I had got rid of my little Fiat when I was in Ghana as it was really too small for long distances. A lovely Triumph Herald took its place and by the time the model I had, a late 1960's version, they had solved all the problems with the half-shafts that they had had. I went to Coventry when I was on leave in the UK to see Mr Triumph and told him I had bought this 1250 and wondered how many half-shafts I should take back to Ghana with me. At this point in the conversation, he pointed to his hair, which was white. I did not quite understand, but actually what he meant was, that was how many problems he had encountered with Triumph Herald half-shafts! He added that all the problems encountered were in his white hair and that these cars were now totally reliable.

'Well, I took this car out to Ghana, sold it at the end of that year when I was due some leave and bought another Triumph Herald, a convertible HKV 780 E in England, used it on that home leave then took it back to Ghana.

'Daphne told me that some people had driven their cars to Timbuktu and she wanted to take a few days off and do the same. It was a long journey and I was not keen; the route would be out of Ghana to Upper Volta, to Bamako and then across the Sahara for a few hundred miles, a round trip from Accra of some 2,500 miles. Anyway, she talked me into it!

'One of the officers who worked with me had a new Peugeot 305 and he didn't want me to go on my own. The helicopter that might have had to come out and rescue us would have cost a lot of money, he said, so this chap and his wife offered to come with us in their Peugeot. Suffice it to say, we all got there without too much trouble and I must say, the route across the desert was almost like a motorway. The desert was sprayed with old fuel oil, a lubricating oil which made the track as hard as could be.

'We found a hotel in Timbuktu run by a lady who had been up to no good in Paris and had decided to retire from her profession and come to this place. Her hotel was becoming a little bit of a centre in Timbuktu but was still fairly quiet and clean. However, other areas around the hotel were not. But we were very lucky and did not suffer from any upset tummies while we were there. We spent a couple of nights at the hotel and then headed back home.

'We had done about a hundred miles when I saw the lights of the Peugeot flashing me. It seemed to be a little further away from us every time I looked. So we had to turn around and head back, a difficult job because of the track and the soft sand all around. Well, his back axle had gone. Luckily, he had a spare one and we were able to jack the car up and rig some sheets over the roof of the car to keep the heat off us. Amazingly, we soon got it sorted out and off we went again. It was very hot and I was astonished that we could get the work done in that heat; it is quite extraordinary how the human body can function when forced to. As you can imagine, this chap was the laughing stock of the wardroom. Everyone had expected the trouble to be with my car, but it wasn't! He was, of course, heart-broken at the trouble we had experienced.

'A real spin-off of this adventure was that the Triumph agent in Ghana was beside himself with happiness; he had an order book full of these Triumphs which people now wanted, having seen how reliable mine was! The Treasury, sadly, would not release the money for him to buy more than one or two of them. I managed to acquire one of these allocations for a nice young officer in the Ghana Navy, a Triumph Herald Estate. Unfortunately, he took it down to the end of the runway at Kotoka Airport. I think he wanted to see how fast it would go, so he level-pegged a Britannia that was taking off. He kept on going as long as he could but should have turned off round a corner at the end of the runway. The plane had already taken off and by then he was doing 70mph! He turned it over. He got it on the road again but it just did not perform the same, and looked pretty awful, too. It was still going at the end of my time in Ghana, a further five years. So, we all had Heralds. We took some pictures and sent them back to Triumph, the whole lot of us outside the Naval Head- quarters, but they were not very interested. I was not surprised, by then, that Britain was loosing their export orders for these types of excellent cars.'

Tom tells us a story about his assistant:

'I think perhaps I should tell you a tale about my assistant, John Rockson. A very handsome young Ghanaian, all the girls loved him, black and white alike. He was sent to Dartmouth and we were horrified to receive a letter from the Captain telling us that he couldn't have Rockson after the end of the next term as he was useless and was holding the rest of the class back. I couldn't understand it. The President couldn't believe it either and ordered him to leave the Navy.

'After a lot of discomfort I went to the Admiral and told him what was being done and asked him to intervene with the President. Reluctantly, he went up that afternoon and by some miracle persuaded the President to give Rockson another chance. He wanted an up-date a year later, but the President had changed and General Ankrah was far more understanding about this chap. He asked me to try and do something with him. Well, Daphne and I took him sailing. I made him stay on in the Dog Watches, thought it would teach him a bit. (Dog Watches are at set times. The first is from 16.00 to 18.00 hours and the second from 18.00 to 20.00.) The Ghanaians didn't think much of sailing, thought it should be left to the fishermen. Rockson, however, liked it and enjoyed his time in our yacht, *Truelove*.'

Tom tells us of one occasion on board the yacht:

'One day, when we were coming back into the harbour at Tema I could see a line squall coming through. The heavens opened and I was a little worried about the fishing boats that were accompanying us. Well, we got back and most of the other boats seemed to be okay except one. Unfortunately, it did not have an engine and appeared to be sinking. We watched from the Control Tower in the Yacht Club and I decided that John could help him, telling him that this was his opportunity to shine. He changed into uniform, commandeered a fishing boat, somehow exercised his authority with everyone on the boat, picked up the three chaps off the sinking boat and even towed it back safely, doing about two knots. They arrived back just before dark.

'I managed to involve the Press and Rockson found himself on the front page of the *Ghanaian Times*. The Admiral was rather impressed with this; it was long after Nkrumah had gone, he was given the Ghanaian DSC, was jolly pleased and stayed in the Navy with the Admiral's consent. He went on to become the Ghanaian Defence Adviser in London and did very well indeed. He ended up pig farming, just west of Accra. I am immensely pleased to think that these people can get on and make a real success with just a little help where necessary.'

*

Chapter 11
Ghana, Ashanti Goldfields
July 1966 to May 1970

Tom knew that his days in Ghana would come to an end:

'By this time, I was beginning to think that I couldn't stay in the Ghana Navy forever. I knew that if I returned to the UK I would have to retire immediately, but I wasn't ready for that yet. A chum of mine, Lt-Cdr Tony Orchard, had retired a little earlier and had a job with the Ashanti Goldfields in Ghana - he was actually the Personal Assistant to General Sir Edward Spears, the Head of the Ashanti Goldfields.

'Tony was always making trips out to Ghana and stayed with us whenever he came over. He wanted to put it to General Spears that I could work for the same chap, maybe even be the Ashanti Goldfields Representative in Ghana, staying close to the President. I asked him who was doing the job at the present time. It was a Colonel Rusty Westmorland. Daphne had been working for him for the last four years and Tony had not said anything to me about it! He said that Rusty wanted to retire and he thought I would be good for the job. He said I could still be in charge of the Ghana Navy Reserve, retaining my interest in the Navy, and I would do very well financially. I said that I needed to think about this and Tony said it depended on whether or not I was able to get on with General and Lady Spears. I had met them before when they had come to Ghana. They came back out a couple of months later and I was invited to go to dinner with them, at Obuasi. Daphne and I drove up in our dear old Triumph and spent the weekend there. Suffice it to say, he said he liked the cut of my jib and told me about the days in the Second World War when he was General de Gaulle's right-hand man. He had written some books on his experiences. One was just being published and he gave me a signed copy of it. He made sure that when I put up for the job, I would get it.

'During this time there had been another coup in Ghana. Some young colonel had taken over the country and we were all pretty fed up; it didn't last long, though, and then there was another coup which got rid of him, also. I am afraid that we were all invited to the ceremony when he was put up against a wall and shot...

'At this time, I put in three month's notice with the Ghana Navy and had to go back to England to select someone to take over my position. I found a nice chap and his lovely wife. So I went back to do the Gibraltar run in the yacht *Ashimota*. It was the first time that we took a Ghanaian as the ship's doctor. We had a charming RN doctor, Surgeon Commander John Lawrence Owen, who was shortly to be appointed to the Royal Yacht and was always on board with us. John assured us that this chap was a good guy to have on board. We fuelled on the way back at Las Palmas and then received a signal from the President to proceed to Monrovia, Liberia, arrange a cocktail party for President Tubman and after that proceed to Ghana with the cargo.

'Monrovia was not a pretty place. I asked this young doctor to make sure that the water was absolutely fit to drink when we took it on board; he assured me he would make a good job of it when he arranged the supply. Unfortunately, he had other things on his mind when he went ashore, girls included, and did not pay much attention to the water. A lot of us went down with hepatitis, one or two of whom did not overcome the illness. The doctor, who was a nephew of one of the Cabinet Ministers, disappeared into northern Ghana, where they would not be able to court-martial him.

'I was, therefore, about to take up my new position from my hospital bed and so did not take the job on in full health at all. The other point which perhaps I should mention here is that on my last leave, while I was still in the Ghana Navy, we had a very important person on board for the Ghana journey from England on *MV Auriol,* a huge 15,000 tonne liner, the flagship of the Elder Dempster line, as I have already mentioned. Just before she sailed I received a telegram from the Admiralty to say that they were sorry they couldn't find anyone to look after His Royal Highness Prince William, Duke of Gloucester. He was only a youngster, going out to Nigeria to take up an appointment with the High Commission in Lagos. I was dead tired by then because we had just bought our house in Clevedon, managed to let it for the time that we would be away and then got ready to go back to Ghana to finish off my job.

'The Prince arrived on board, he was lovely. Just the sort of chap you didn't mind keeping an eye on. Wherever we went, he knew everyone. They even put up a Dakota to escort us in at Monrovia. When we got to Tema we parted company; he said he would come back to stay some weekends with us. In fact, he did - he got fed up with Lagos and came to stay with us quite often. He had his own aeroplane and flew straight into the airport, then would play some polo. Later, the Duke flew an aircraft back from the UK. We lost radar contact with it in some remote part of Liberia; he had run out of petrol and landed on an old airstrip. The locals, who hadn't seen an aeroplane since the war, had a spot of bother trying to find some petrol for it!

'Anyhow, I am diverting from the Ghana Navy and my own move from there to work for the Ashanti Goldfields. General Ankrah asked me to keep an eye on the Ghana Naval Reserve, and I said I would. I soon got into the way of the job as it was not really very different from what I was already doing with the

Navy. I had to deal with the President of the Ghana Commercial Bank; in my previous position I had asked the bank for money to buy ships; this way round, I was giving them gold for their banks!

'I had been doing the Ashanti job for a couple of years, until about 1968, when one afternoon the Telex rang. It was a message from Lady Spears, asking me if I was on my own. When I said I was, she told me that Tiny Rowlands of Lhonro had been in touch with the President, proposing to buy the Ashanti Goldfields, give half to the Government of Ghana and keep the other half for Lhonro. The Spears had been in touch with Tiny Rowlands asking him to confirm that this was the action he wanted to take. They wanted me to go and see General Ankrah about this, so I phoned his PA and arranged a meeting. When I saw the general he was a bit coy, but admitted that he had been approached by Tiny Rowlands. The outcome was that the Ashanti Goldfields were taken over by Lhonro.

'Spears was a very interesting chap who spoke perfect French. When the war came he got out of France with General De Gaulle, was appointed his Aide and Deputy and became the main link between France and the UK. He had a terribly important role to play with *HMS Bulolo* during the North African landings, when Admiral Darlan was in Algiers. The admiral was hopping mad at the Royal Navy for sinking his ships. Spears went with De Gaulle and pacified him, as a result of which we managed to take the rest of the French fleet without a single shot being fired.

'On another trip in *Bulolo*, the French became upset with the British in Casablanca Harbour. As we came in, we asked one of the chaps to have a word with the French ships. Well, the more our chap talked in French on the loud speaker, the more we could see the French ships reacting adversely.

Someone eventually sorted it out, but it made me realise that not everyone liked De Gaulle, especially the French Navy!' Tom returns to the more peaceful activities he was able to enjoy:

'Sailing was still my special interest when I was in Ghana. I did all I could to get the young Ghanaian officers and ratings involved, as well as looking after the Tema Yacht Club. My boat, *Truelove*, the Folk Boat I mentioned before, was kept at the Yacht Club. It was a lovely wooden boat, beautifully designed. We also had a couple of 14-foot Internationals, and two Naval dinghies about the same length.

'I was in one of these Internationals one afternoon and was determined to win the race. There was another guy, in the RAF, who was as equally determined that I wouldn't win! We went around the first lap just about even. I needed to tack a little further inshore on the next lap and then I would be okay. Well, I mistook some of the leading marks and I was just about in the surf and in trouble, being pounded around with my assistant, Lieutenant John Rockson. We tried to go about just as the first wave was beginning to break; just got around, but it was very close indeed. We won the race but were very lucky to do so.'

Truelove was a major part of Tom's life really:

'I took *Truelove* out every Sunday. I had a Ghanaian boatman, Joe, who always had the boat ready, and Daphne and I would take some food along with us. For Joe, it was the only decent meal he had all week! Then we went out and got our fish. On Christmas Day, we decided to try to go as far towards the Equator as we could, but couldn't, it was a good 60 miles. I hope that Joe realised that I wasn't coming back to Ghana as I didn't have the opportunity to sell the boat before we left. I hope he sold it and kept the money.

'By then a President from the Armed Forces had been superseded by a civil government under Doctor Busia. Busia was a lovely man and did his utmost to get the country up together, but life did not improve, so ultimately, the Ghanaians went back to having someone from the Armed Forces as President, a chap called Jerry Rawlins, who is still there now.

'Rawlins was quite ruthless. There were many good officers I thought a lot of who went to the firing squad. But I think he probably did the right thing; he went to the grass roots of the problem: anyone who was up to any reasonable amount of trouble was made an example of. It brought about a new Ghana. They know the mistakes they have made and the Queen's recent visit was a great event. The country has not improved a lot economically, but it is a very honourable country now. If Flight-Lieutenant Jerry Rawlins had taken on the job earlier, I might still be there now! Who knows. I remember him at the Officers Training Establishment at Teshie, where he was almost a joke. Red haired and with a pale skin. But he became a great fighter pilot and Ghana could not have done better than have this chap as their leader.'

To return to Tom's initial problems:

'I was in the UK on leave when I received news that my entry permit would not be renewed. My wife had not been well on the last tour in Ghana; she had had an hysterectomy during the leave trip and was convalescing when I heard this, but she was allowed to go back and sort out our affairs. She flew back and did very well, selling the car. But she couldn't get the badge off the car, the Bristol Light Car Club, it just would not come off and I was very disappointed with that. We also managed to remove our money out of Ghana, which wasn't easy at all. But there it was, we were out of Ghana. The guy who relieved me, we were never good friends, had been a general under Mr Smith in Rhodesia.'

154

Daphne returned to the UK:

'My wife came back in the *RMS Auriol*, soon after which the ship came out of service when the Elder Dempster line, who said they could not continue the service to the West Coast of Africa. They finished about 1971, but *RMS Auriol* went on making trips to Southampton. It provided a good service but more and more of the Government people were going by air. The Britannia had come into its own and provided a very reliable service for Ghana Airways. The only Britannia pilot (an Ace) that I knew was an ex-RAF Wing-Commander, Andrew Evans, who had been in charge of flying a Catalina Squadron during the war. I was drinking with him one night when we heard about a terrible tragedy; an Acquila Air Ways plane en route to the Canary Islands had hit a hill on the Isle of Wight. Evans told me about a fuel switch that sat over your head in the cockpit. It looked very similar to the switch that altered the air conditioning, and is next door to it; however, it turns off the fuel supply. Well, this chap had turned the wrong switch off and so the plane had lost its fuel supply, gone out of control and met a nasty end. This reminded me of a night in Ghana.

'We lived at the end of the airstrip at Kotoka Airport and were sitting out having our Horlicks or some other bedtime drink. We heard this chap revving up the 11 o'clock Britannia. Suddenly there was a terrible row as he put all four engines in reverse, even though he was nearing the end of the runway. There was no bang, or anything obvious that the plane had been on a collision course at all, just this awful racket. Then silence as it slowly taxied back to the start. It did not fly that night.

'Wing-Commander Evans told me he had just had enough. The pilot had made the decision that the maximum weight of the plane had been exceeded and, as the captain has every right to do, decided not to fly the aircraft. It seemed that he just could not leave the ground, and when it was weighed it was over a thousand pounds overweight! Evans had a little sports car in Ghana and another one at Heathrow!'

Tom relates why his visa was not renewed, hence his departure from Ghana:

'In the Spring of 1970 we held our usual cocktail party prior to proceeding on summer leave from Ghana. It was a very happy evening, attended by many of the Cabinet Ministers in Dr Busia's government. A senior official produced a cigarette packet, wrote a number on the back of it and asked me to arrange for the firm in the UK who were doing some large-scale work for the Navy to place the usual gratuity payments in this special account with the relevant bank, the number of which he had given me on the packet.

'I was surprised to hear myself say "I am sorry sir, I cannot do it." He replied that he knew that I had had a long, busy and very successful year and was now very tired, but this was important. However, I stood my ground. He was obviously annoyed with my reaction, replying "All right then, don't bother to return here after your leave."

'Well, Daphne and I spent the first couple of days of our leave, after her hospitalisation, at the Royal Pier Hotel, Weston-super-Mare. The phone rang on the second day, in the middle of our afternoon siesta. The Ghana High Commissioner was ringing me to say that he had received a telex to say that Commander Foden's entry visa was not to be renewed. He was very pleasant and said he realised this was a mistake and when would I be able to come to the High Commission in London to have a spot of lunch and get it renewed. It appeared that my friend at the cocktail party had been as good as his word. We went home from the hotel that night and contacted

Sir Edward and Lady Spears. I then realised what wonderful friends I had in this couple.

'There was an editorial in the Daily Telegraph, Monday 27 July 1970 about this incident, and a lot of diplomatic activity, with howls of protest from the Ghana press, too! I spent a few days at the London office of Ashanti Goldfields, but having been taken over by Lhonro a replacement for me had been found. General Alexander was nominated, successfully, for my job. The general had been the Head of Mr Smith's Army in Rhodesia but he and Mr Smith parted company when the troubles there flared up. He was a good friend of Lhonro, but not of mine.

'The official reason for my departure was some tale that I had been spying for the British, using a special radio. It was true that I had a radio, but it was a single, side-band set for use between Accra and the Ashanti Goldfields at Obuasi. The radio proved its worth when there was a lightning strike at the mine and I was able to obtain the Ghana Army's assistance very quickly, obviating any serious damage to either personnel or equipment. But that's another story.

'With the exception of Boris the Samoyed, mentioned in Chapter Five, I have not mentioned the animals in my life. We had various cats in Malta but it was not until Ghana that we really had any special animals. When we arrived, an RN officer who was returning to the UK on completion of his service there asked us if we would take on a year-old black and white farm cat and a year-old Siamese, otherwise they would have to be destroyed as there were no other takers. We reluctantly agreed, but soon realised what good companions they were.

'When we had people in for drinks in the evening the cats would liven up the proceedings by playing on the lawn, or sometimes chasing each other on to the roof. However, they really earned their pay when on two occasions we had a near miss with snakes. We had returned from a meal with friends about 22.30 and were having a night cap on the veranda. All around was heavy foliage. Suddenly, close to my right shoulder there was frightful commotion. The farm cat had bitten a cobra in the neck and killed it as it was about to spit at me. Sadly, the cat had got the snake's poison in his left eye. We rushed him off to our friendly Ghanaian vet, an excellent man who lived about a mile away. Fortunately, he was in, and immediately got some very scarce fresh milk from the fridge and bathed the cat's eye. Together with an antibiotic injection, he saved the cat's life, but his eye was never quite the same again.

'The vet warned us that the snake's mate would probably have a go at one of us and to take great care for a few days. Sure enough, the very next night almost the same thing happened and Bruno (the Siamese) killed the snake. But he was a split second quicker than his chum and the snake was unable to spit its poison before Bruno killed it.

'Well, you can imagine, we felt that we had a great debt to these two animals and decided we would bring then home to Clevedon when we finally left Ghana. We had them inoculated against goodness knows what and they left Ghana by KLM, via Amsterdam, for Bristol, to be met by the lady who would take them into quarantine for 6 months. But it was not to be. They had to spend a few days at KLM's animal sanctuary in Amsterdam, because no animals were allowed into the U.K. for a week owing to a rabies scare. Somehow, they both caught cat 'flu, almost unknown in Ghana, so they were not inoculated against it. KLM's veterinary facilities in Amsterdam were excellent, all that could be done was done, but sadly both animals died a few days later. KLM returned all the fares, with a full letter of explanation and a letter of sympathy.

'A few weeks later, after we had got over the tragedy, I set about buying Daphne another animal and was recommended to

Mrs Kidd of Brindsey, near Congresbury, who not only liked Burmese cats but was a well known animal show judge. She recommended we went to a lady near Reading where, after some investigation, we bought a Burmese male cat, using the compensation money from KLM. I kept all the negotiations secret from my wife and it was quite a surprise to her and did her a lot of good. We went up to Reading to take possession of the delightful animal. It was raining all the way back to Clevedon and Shan, as he was called, spent most of the time pawing at the windscreen wipers. He transformed my wife's life, went everywhere with her and was first in the car when we were going anywhere.

'We were very lucky in having charming neighbours. The lady suffered from asthma and had a small dog. Shan and the dog never really saw eye to eye. One day, they came for drinks and the lady was delighted Shan was not to be seen in our sitting room, remarking that she would have no trouble with her asthma. As soon as she left Shan appeared from behind the curtains! Can some of these health problems be somewhat in the mind, I ask?!

'The next event involving Shan was funny but could have been catastrophic. Our neighbours, who had been with us in Ghana, bought the lower part of our house from us. He was a senior Foreign Office diplomat and often had his friends down from London for the weekend. On this occasion it was the Japanese Ambassador, who was very partial to good red meat. Some super beef-steak cutlets were obtained from Clevedon's best butcher and were prepared for that evening's dinner. For some reason, this included being placed by the open kitchen window. All this was carefully observed by Shan, in the garden bushes some twenty yards away. For a few moments, the kitchen was left unoccupied. Shan saw his chance and somehow made off with all the meat. Great consternation in the galley. Shan was suspected and I was informed.

'In one of my few flashes of sense, I said that fortunately we were also having steak and I would bring it down. Frenzied activity while I endeavoured to find some steak in the bottom of our deep freeze. I managed to find some, which had been in there for about a year, ever since our last year's leave, and immediately placed it under hot water.

'Next morning, I enquired how the dinner party had gone. To my amazement and relief, I was told the steak was super. They enquired where I had purchased it from? I didn't dare tell them from a little Clevedon butcher, about a year ago!

'We had a relatively quiet and happy time with Mr Shan for some years. I think he was very sad when my first wife died of cancer in 1980. I remarried in 1984 and was very worried how the animal would treat his new mistress but in a few months they were great friends.

'All was well until one night in 1985. About 03.00 hours I heard a faint 'meow' in the vicinity of the back door cat flap. I knew it was not Shan and rushed downstairs to see what was going on, yelling to my wife not to touch any cats should they come up to our bedroom. As I went down the stairs the cat who had strayed into our house rushed past me, followed by Shan. I grabbed a jug of water and rushed up behind them, too late to stop Shan commencing to quietly dispose of the other animal. Joan could not bear this and before I could throw the water at the pair of them, she attempted to separate them. Fatal. Shan bit right through her arm and we had to go to Clevedon's cottage hospital at about 03.45. The next day Shan knew he had done a dreadful thing and could not leave Joan alone. I asked the vet if he should be put down but was told certainly not, he was only protecting his home from intruders.

'I could go on and on about this animal and his exploits on board the *Balmoral* and *Waverley* but suffice it to say he had an interesting life! He died in 1989 aged 18, which, for a thoroughbred, was very good. We all shed a tear, including the very senior vet who must have been so used to despatching terminally ill animals.'

*

Chapter 12
The Imperial Ethiopian Navy
May 1970 to May 1975

'I had hoped that my little problem with the authorities in Ghana would go unnoticed but somehow the *Daily Telegraph* got to hear that Tom Foden was being asked not to return to Ghana. When I picked up the phone one morning it was the *Daily Telegraph* saying they wanted to send a reporter to see me about these goings on. When the chap turned up he had all the facts about it in front of him. Well, the next day, there it was on the front page, the tragedy of Tom Foden not being able to return to Ghana. And in the Editorial, too. It didn't do much for Ghana, I can tell you. It later appeared in all the other papers.

'I hoped it would all be forgotten but three days later I received another call, this time from His Imperial Highness, Rear Admiral Prince Alexander Desta. He was the Deputy Commander of the small but very strategically important Ethiopian Navy. The Commander, of course, was the Emperor. I had had the honour of training the prince when I was with the RN Coastal Forces at *HMS Hornet*, and again saw a lot of him when he was serving in destroyers based in Malta. We lent him our flat there for his 21st Birthday party. I believe Birkikara Street, Sliema talked about it for years after! Anyway, the prince said he was coming to see me. He had a contract in his pocket and wanted me to be part of the Ethiopian Navy!

'I had planned to see Mr Robert Hoddle, a senior partner of Alonso, Dawson, Hoddle, a well known North Somerset estate agents, thinking I could manage with the various pensions I had collected and would buy a small farm on the Mendips where I could grow turkeys and live in peace thereafter. Anyway, Alexander arrived in his E-Type Jaguar absolutely certain that he had me marked up for his Navy. He said he was seeing Admiral Lord Lewin (then the First Sea Lord) the very next day and he didn't want to tell him that Tom Foden had turned down the job as his deputy in the Ethiopian Navy.

'Well, we discussed the matter for several hours, during which time we consumed a great deal of wine and ate dinner. Then he produced the contract and that was that. My wife was not terribly happy, even though we all knew each other pretty well. I had a few months before I had to take up the appointment and found myself going out to Addis Ababa and then Asmara around November time, a nice part of the year there. They had some very nice hotels and I enjoyed the country very much.

'The Ethiopians are desperately honest people. I remember one occasion when we came back to the UK in the early 1970's. I arrived with the Head of Stores, Ato Tewolde, and we looked in on Mr Gieves (known as Gieves and Hawkes). He took me to one side and said he thought that Ato's suit was a bit frayed and suggested that he would get him another one after lunch. Well, later on Ato was looking a little red-faced and worried and told me that Mr Gieves had tried to bribe him by getting him a suit, which would be charged to the company and not to him! They were terribly honest; you could never give them anything that could be misconstrued as a bribe.

'The first time I went out to Ethiopia the chap in charge of the accommodation at Massawa was not keen on my taking the job and put me in some terrible quarters. Alexander Desta came down from the Naval HQ in Addis Ababa, was appalled with the conditions and I was quickly moved to a rather more resplendent place, with two servants. I said to Alexander

Desta that I had thought the chap had done it as a bit of a joke and could we just forget it.

'I must say Desta, eldest grandson of His Imperial Majesty the Emperor Haile Selassie I, was just the most charming gentleman you could possibly meet. He knew everyone, and along with that was more English than the English! He had been to a good English Prep School in Bath, then to Wellington, followed by Dartmouth, and had then served in the Royal Navy. I do feel that if things had gone on as they were we would still be living there.

'I had a book of Air Vouchers that you just filled in when you wanted to travel. The Ethiopian Airlines were excellent and the senior pilots were Americans, really terribly efficient. To start with they only went as far as Rome and Paris but by the time I left they were flying to Heathrow.'

At this point, Tom explains why there was an Ethiopian Navy:

'You may ask why there was an Ethiopian Navy; a lot of people have asked me that! These little countries, after the war, liked to have their own navy. The French were mixed up in this quite a bit, they mainly had French Officers in their Commands. When I went there the captain of *HIMS Ethiopia*, His Imperial Majesty's Ship, their Flagship, had a French Officer in command. They started this little navy when Alexander Desta left the Royal Navy. It was strategically very important and had up to the minute technology; they knew exactly what was going on under the water, as well as on top.

'When Desta went back into the Imperial Ethiopian Navy he soon got things going. He knew everything and everybody and was known all over the world. Many countries sent a ship to the annual Imperial Navy Days and everybody had a good time together. It was a very well respected service in the Red Sea, almost like a branch of the Royal Navy: nearly all the officers had gone through Dartmouth and if not, to a British university. This did, however, create some problems, a mutiny of the Armed Forces actually, as some of these officers did not go to Oxford or Cambridge but to lesser known universities where communism had set in, and when they came back to the Ethiopian Armed Forces they were riddled with the disease.'

Tom explains further about the Imperial Ethiopian Navy:

'In the Fleet we had *HIMS Ethiopia,* a large ex-American destroyer, and various other ships including minesweepers from the Royal Navy. We used to go up and down the Red Sea keeping a special eye on the Russian interests there and in the Suez Canal. We used various methods to carry out this task.

'Ethiopian Navy days, which used to take place every February, were the *Raison d'etre,* to outsiders, for our being there. Amazingly, we spent the whole year getting ready for them. Alexander Desta used to take trips to the UK to Selfridges and Harrods to buy things for these days and we overdid it a bit. The last exercise, before the tragedy of the coup, was actually bringing in tourists.

'A few of my friends from Clevedon came out and stayed in Asmara in a beautiful hotel, and came along to our various parties. We had the Royal Marines Band come and play and Princess Anne also visited. It wasn't easy for her as she had come straight from the UK. The climate was warm and if you weren't used to it, you needed a day or two to settle down; she got a little bit of tummy trouble and the Medical Officer of the Royal Yachts didn't seem to prescribe the right drug. However, our French Medical Officer took over and gave her something else and all was well. We had the Flag Officer Royal Yachts out as well, Rear-Admiral Trowbridge, and also Captain David Loram from *HMS Antrim,* the British ship. I had to brief him about the Ethiopian Navy. The whole occasion excelled beyond everything we thought it would. The

Royal Marines Band concert was just magnificent, something, I shall never forget. I went to one recently on board *HMS Invincible* which stirred the same emotions as the band did then. Just shows you that when the Royal Marines try there is nothing in the World that can beat them!

'These Navy Days lasted a few days and on the final day, the Emperor, as Admiral Commander-in-Chief of all the Forces, came out in *HMIS Ethiopia* and we had exercises all day with all the nationalities doing the drills together the whole day long. It showed how they could all get on together. All the crews went ashore together in the evenings, saw the young ladies that they shouldn't see and had a jolly good time, so they worked hard and played hard!'

Tom lets us know a little bit about the Emperor:

'He was a dear man but you had to know what you were doing with him. I hadn't been in Ethiopia very long when Prince Alexander suggested that he present me to his grandfather - and that I would have to leave his presence walking backwards. He said I would have to speak in French. My audience was for 10 o'clock on the following Tuesday. I polished my shoes, wore my Ethiopian Navy kit, looked pretty smart really. The Emperor spoke perfect French and I replied the very best that I could. He asked me how I felt about being in Ethiopia and said he remembered his days in Bath. I managed to get out backwards without falling over!

'A nice gesture the Emperor made was that everyone of Commander level or above was given a little tie clip made from the Emperor's gold fashioned in the model of *HIMS Ethiopia*. I was very honoured to receive this. When I got my clip, he spoke in perfect English, and even asked my advice about buying a new ship to guard the Coast against smugglers! I was in a difficult position because I knew that Alexander needed such a ship badly, but they were very poor people and it was difficult to suggest anything at all, let alone newer, faster boats. We both went to see the Emperor about the boat and I knew that Alexander wanted me to agree with him, which I did, the Emperor saying he would buy a ship when there were more tourists bringing currency into the country. I still have the tie clip, a most excellent keep-sake.'

Tom tells us of the living quarters and life in Ethiopia:

'Conditions in Ethiopia for the Royal Navy, the Army and the RAF Officers who were seconded out there were, on the whole, pretty good. I said that to start with, my accommodation was terrible, but I soon received some much more comfortable quarters. I had an excellent steward and an excellent cook and when I returned to the UK these ratings went back to the wardroom.

'There were quite a few married quarters with WRENs in them who were married to Ethiopian servicemen. These quarters were the A1 of Ethiopian married quarters, nearly about the same as the ones we have for junior officers here in the UK. There was a reasonable but not extensive social life. There were one or two Engineer officers and some WREN officers and one or two commercial guys, as well, so between us all we had quite a lot of fun. We had something going on almost every night. It was a fast pace but economical.

'We didn't have the facilities that we had had in Ghana, or the money that we had had there. People seemed to own old bangers brought out by the Ethiopian Shipping Company who were very good at doing this sort of thing. We had a very well known ex-Royal Navy training Captain, Beatty, VC. The training establishment was on the hills behind Massawa and there were facilities there to do up these cars. A few months later, they would reappear like new. This was how the Ethiopians had existed right from the times of the Queen of

Sheba. They were wonderful at repair work. By the way, the Emperor Haile Selassie I was a direct descendant of hers.

'Things were quite fun and done with a minimum of expense, which I liked, because the country was so very, very poor. Not as bad as it is now. I refuse to even watch these Aid programmes, let alone give them anything. The more aid they get the less likely they are to get back to their old traditions. They have managed to get by without an emperor for a long time but they all believe that their Emperor was a direct descendant from the One Above.

'It was very sad when, gradually, the communists took over the Army, which they did by seducing their officers in the UK. The Army chaps who had been infiltrated with communism started to mutiny a couple of months ahead of the Navy Days in 1975, and by the time these activities were completed they were ready to take the Navy over. They moved down towards Massawa, the big Navy Base. We were very well informed about what was going on and how long it would be before they reached the Isthmus where the Base was. I was very naïve, thinking that a few shells would stop them. When it came to it, I went to Alexander Desta and reassured him that there wouldn't really be much trouble and showed him where a few shells would hurt them most. Alexander, however, said he would never be party to killing any of his brothers, and would not have any shells fired. He wanted to do it by negotiation. He said that he was taking the WRENs, his staff and myself to Djibouti, from where we would go on a scheduled flight to Addis Ababa. Sadly, many of these WRENs, who were now married to Ethiopian Officers, would not come. The rest took a minesweeper and went overnight down to Djibouti.

'I had thought that I would not go as I didn't really want to leave all my gear in the quarter. Neither did I wish to leave my Volkswagen VW! Alexander said that he could not guarantee my safety and thought I was a complete fool. So, they went off and I stayed the night in my quarter. I was awakened by a soldier from one of the Ethiopian Regiments; I told him I was staying in my Quarters. I said that if there was any kind of rough play towards our people, I was directly in communication with the navy, who would be able to put a stop to it. He suggested that I speak to the Mutineers' Tribunal.

'They knew I was a friend of the Admiral's. I had a document from the Navy so that in this sort of situation I could produce it. I repeated the same message: that no harm should come to the remaining Naval Staff and that *Antrim*, which was lying off, would come forward and support us. I told them that I was staying there, which I did. I then went for a swim in the pool - and had a mutineer with a gun trained on me the whole time!

'Gradually, these people took over the Base. They did not have much Intelligence because the Ethiopian Navy ratings did not give them very much assistance. The star in all of this was the French Surgeon Commander, who was a great chap. His father had been killed by the British during the war as we thought he was a spy, but he never let it interfere with his work. The French are very good in these circumstances. The Admiralty didn't keep the *Antrim* on station and it went on its way, but the French kept their destroyer there, which was a huge deterrent. The French were quite definite in saying that if any Contract officers were harmed in any way the destroyer would fire at the Base. I informed the twelve WRENs of this to reassure them.

'I was the senior of the ex-Pat officers but we had an Indian Officer with us who said he was more senior. We looked up the Navy List which gives the seniority of our RN and Commonwealth Officers and found that he really was junior to me. I was mad with this officer as he had made me give way before on other matters.

'I told the Communists that harm would come to them if they upset our Staff, and suggested that the RN courses would stop also. This was the bit that they so enjoyed, a few weeks back in the UK, undergoing training. They gradually came around to common sense.

'Admiral Desta resigned. Another chap with only slight communist leanings was appointed in his place. I told him I wanted to go back to the UK. He asked me to stay for a while longer and then go back to the UK to the universities and explain what had happened to their officers - and also to stop various contracts. I had a chat with Admiral Alexander and he suggested that it would be good for me to go. The new Commodore-in-Command said that I was free to leave the Base. I thought that I would go to Asmara, do one or two things there, then see if I could get back to the UK. One of the Ethiopian Officers said that there was a bus once a day to Asmara. He suggested that I go in uniform, so my cap badge was swapped for a Royal Navy one. I managed to get out of the Base, went to a ramshackle office, booked a seat on a bus and got to Asmara.

'I immediately went to the British Consul, who said there was no air traffic going back to the UK. I went to an hotel where the Ethiopian Navy had an account and I where I knew I could stay. The Consul said that he would let the Foreign Office know. Next, I went to the Navy contingent that we had in Asmara and was briefed as to what I could do on their behalf when I got back to the UK.

'With all that had gone on I was overdue arriving in UK by three weeks and my wife was a bit hot under the collar about it. But she had been to see an old chum at the Foreign Office, who had been the High Commissioner in Ghana, and he had done some research with the Embassy at Addis Ababa who, in turn, had got in touch with the Consul at Asmara who had told them I was okay. But I was missing out on some important meetings back home regarding trained of officers and the purchase of stores, all of which I wished to attend.

'Anyway, there I was, wandering around in Asmara and quite safe. It was extraordinary that in the middle of this awful coup, I was elsewhere in a nice, quiet city.

'Another chum of mine there was the Immigration Officer; he came to the hotel one night and told me that a Britannia aircraft was in, loaded with tomatoes from an organisation called Meridian Airways. It was in for some work on the engines but would be ready to go in a couple of days. He suggested I just get on this plane, no questions asked.

'Next, I bumped into the captain of the plane who was staying in another hotel. I thought that I had seen him before and it turned out he had been one of the pilots I had served with in Lossiemouth! He said that he would give me a lift back to the UK but said it would be a bit risky and that I would have to walk out to the plane in uniform with the rest of the crew. If we were counted and they found that there was one more person than there should be, I would have to laugh it off as I could.

'The decided to leave the next evening. There was no question of stamping passports, you just don't do it for a crew of a ship or an aeroplane. Anyway, the engines started, the instruments were checked and we were ready for take off. We got airborne and then all of a sudden, on the RT, the Control Officer from the control tower informed us that they knew we had eight people on board and that there should only be seven. The Captain very coolly replied that he would get the First Officer to check the plane. We waited for some time and Asmara then asked if we had checked; and when we said no, they demanded that we return. However, the Captain told them it was not possible, as the hydraulics on the plane had been the problem before, and a trip back would not do the plane any good. Luckily, we were nearly out of their range; they had threatened to send up fighter planes to intercept us.

'We had problems of our own. The hydraulics were in a mess and the Flight Engineer was fighting with the panel of instruments and wiring, trying to get them to work; we couldn't land in the state that we were in. Eventually he got the hydraulics working. We went quietly on our way to Jedda, where we had to refuel.

'This Airline always refuelled there, it was much cheaper. We came into land, nice landing, taxied up to the fuel depot, Shell Company, and asked the Duty Officer to come along and arrange refuelling. He came along quickly enough and immediately asked the Captain if he was going to pay his debts. The chap said that we would be on the runway for a long time if we didn't pay up. We put our heads together and collected about a couple of hundred pounds, enough to pay for the fuel that we wanted for this trip. Reluctantly, he did refuel us but now we were all out of money! The Captain said that we should be able to get directly to Stansted on the fuel that we had provided we managed to get into a Jet Stream and turned off two of the engines. It was not a straight line that we were going in, but it would be a pretty direct trip.

'When we got closer to Stanstead, the Captain said that our Radar wasn't working; Stanstead replied that theirs wasn't working either. We approached, lower and lower, a little mist was settling too. We saw the Landing Lights and the Captain put the plane down a little heavily. One of the tyres burst but the tomatoes were fine and were sold in Covent Garden the very next day.

'The Purser of the plane gave me a lift so that I could get the last train from Paddington to Bristol. I got to Paddington with seven minutes to spare. My wife met me at Bristol Parkway. We were both very pleased to see each other after such a time apart!'

Tom was so pleased to be home but he had his work cut out:

'Over the next few months I was busy arranging the next guys for Dartmouth. The new Commodore asked me to just go ahead and arrange everything as normal, so I did. It was early Spring and I was desperately in need of some leave. I wanted to ask the Commodore for a month off before we did any more arrangements. I gave the Commodore a call in Ethiopia and he approved my leave.

'Well, my flat mate in our house in Clevedon, Alex Birch, Advisor to the President of Antigua, said that he would very much like to see us anytime, so I called him as well. He was pleased to think that we would visit him. We went out and were very relaxed for a while and then one day a telegram turned up for me: it was very sad news. Prince Alexander, in Ethiopia, had been shot, along with about thirty others. The Emperor had also been smothered, although they didn't say that at the time.

'I wrote my resignation straight away. I just didn't want anything to do with it. There was no prospect of anything getting back to normal out there. I actually asked two of my chums, Naval chaps, to forward my resignation to Ethiopia as I was determined to never go near the place again until proper order had been restored by whoever should take over from the Emperor. To me, someone had to be restored to the throne, for without someone on the throne starvation, poverty and chaos would be rife. Up until then, starvation had never been a scene of Ethiopia, but it was there now.

'The direct descendant has a good car establishment in the north of England and should be reinstated. He is also the head of the Rastafarians and they all believe that he should be put on the throne again. Their belief is that the reigning monarch is a direct descendant of 'Our Lord Above'.

'When I left Massawa, there were some WRENs still living with their Ethiopian husbands but I couldn't say what happened to them. They had been protected by us up until then. A long time later, I heard that the French Surgeon Commander at the Naval Hospital made sure that they didn't come to any harm. By then, there weren't any Royal Navy personnel there at all, so I was about the last to leave. I was very sad to leave the Navy, but it had to be.'

Tom's life took yet another turn:

'I was phoned by a senior Minister in the government who told me that there would be a Memorial Service for Prince Alexander and the other thirty senior officers who had been shot. They wanted me to be an usher. On the day, among others present there was a very young Winston Churchill (grandson of Sir Winston). So I was amongst some very fine people that day.

'The Ethiopians were so law abiding, I found it extraordinary that any one man could carry out such a massacre. History might have been very different if this had not happened.

*

Chapter 13
The Royal Naval Auxiliary Service
the MV Balmoral and PS Waverley
May 1975 to the present time

'For the first time in my life, I did not have a job. It did not worry me financially, but it did worry me psychologically! It was early 1976 and I didn't want to retire as I felt sure that I would really hate it.

'The Navy had always been good to me and I started to use contacts from my Ghana days. Luckily, there was a chap, Captain John Murray, who had rather an interesting job lined up for me. He was then head of the Royal Naval Auxiliary Service and he needed someone to run the operation, working out of the Bristol Channel.

'The Admiralty recruited more than 50% of retired Merchant Navy ratings and other Navy ratings for various duties around our coastline and inland. Basically, they needed people who were already trained in the ways of the sea.

'The Royal Navy Auxiliary Service flew a Blue Ensign defaced by an exploding bomb in water. Their task was to assist the Royal Navy in identifying mines laid and bombs dropped in port areas in the UK and overseas, and to assist the RN in conveying personnel and stores to ships at anchor.'

Tom really was unsure about taking the position:

'When I was originally offered the job I said I was completely out of touch and really would like a couple of months off, but they were desperate to find someone do the job, so I took it. They were a nice lot to work with and I was paid expenses, as well as a quarter of my Naval pay. It was supposed to be about twenty hours work a week but I didn't see how it could be as little as that; the work involved a great geographical area stretching over the West of England and Wales.

'However, the work was quite fun, and I did enjoy it. People used to meet in the evening and I would see what they were up to and make sure that they were on the right track. It was a fairly free and easy set up; there was not so much discipline in the Auxiliary Service as I had experienced in the RNR. We did, however, manage to whip this lot up to a fairly high standard; they even played a part in the Queen's visit to Bristol. These chaps needed a bit of drilling for that visit! As the years went by I think we made them a little bit smarter in all sorts of ways.

'Our fleet included a couple of Fleet Tenders, little ships about 120 feet long, the *Loyal Chancellor* and *Loyal Moderator*, very useful indeed for carrying personnel and stores to much bigger Naval ships that might be lying off Portbury. They could also carry stores and depth charges if they had to. We used to do a run to Gloucester Docks through the Sharpness Canal and then back to Barry Island.'

In fact, Tom, needless to say, had a near miss on one of these particular runs:

'On one trip I called up the Dockmaster at Avonmouth to let them know where we were. This was a fairly routine event, nothing spectacular; we were still some distance from Bristol Docks, making for Avonmouth itself. However, the Dockmaster, whom I knew quite well by then, thought we were quite mad. We had no idea what the weather was doing as our forecast when we left Gloucester had been quite good; however, we were in the lee of the shore and did not know that the forecast was now reporting a Force 8-9 gale! Anyway, the Dockmaster was not going to allow us to enter Avonmouth at first but said he would leave the lock gates open as long as he could. We arrived just as they were being shut. I attempted to go ashore but it was impossible even to stand up in that wind. It was a very narrow escape. One of many, I fear, that occur in the Channel.'

This was not the only work that Tom was offered at that time:

'Meanwhile, my next-door neighbour in Edgehill Road, Clevedon, was the Chairman of a small Shipping Company called P & A Campbell. He suggested that if I was not over-burdened with my present work he would like me to look after his ships when they were in the Bristol area. This was nothing new; I had served with these P & A Campbell ships in the summers when I had been in Ethiopia. I managed to do this because the Ethiopian Navy gave us so much time off. Well, I was also doing some work for the magazine Navy International, run by Commodore Ray Hart whom I had worked with in Haslemere. So I was pretty flat out with three jobs! '

However, the three jobs changed:

'Things started to fall apart a bit! The Navy International business was sold, making us a little bit of lolly. Also, I was finding the Auxiliary Service a strain as my wife had developed cancer and I needed more and more time to be with her. She died soon after I had given up the job. So, sadly, I had to resign. The Auxiliary Service were very good, they understood and anyway I was over the age limit. Not many Officers served over the age of 65. P & A was sold to European Ferries, which was part of P & O! P & O weren't too bothered about keeping P & A either, so they decided to close it down at the end of that year, 1981. The Auxiliary Service was the first part of the Navy to be pensioned off, but it was the right thing to do and I had left it by then anyway. The Service ran from 1965 to 1983.

'At the end of that year, one of the group that I worked with received a phone call from someone who had a paddle steamer called the *Waverley,* the last sea-going passenger paddle-steamer in the world. He thought the Bristol Channel would be a good place to try it out. So, Captain David Neill of the *Waverley* came down to see what it was like taking a steamer up the River Avon.

'We had the *MV Balmoral* there, the only ship we had left, but it suited us to demonstrate on the river, so we went up it the next day. The owner of the *Balmoral* was not too happy at the prospect of this other chap showing an interest in either the *Balmoral* or bringing another steamer to the area, so we took Captain Neill on a trip up the river. He understood from that trip that some parts of the Channel were pretty difficult; such as a notorious spot, the Horseshoe Bend. He liked the idea of bringing this steamer to the Channel and reckoned that with a little charity money coming in the following year he would be able to try the *Waverley* out in the Channel for a while. He also needed a Captain for his little steamer and wanted to use one of the ex-Captains who was, obviously, used to Paddle Steamers and could come and spend a couple of days with him.

'All was set for the following year. Everyone was mad keen to start this project as we were all aware that it would be a jolly good tourist attraction. So, the following year the little steamer came to us for a whole six weeks. We managed to get hold of Captain George Gunn, from Swansea, to assist Neill.'

Tom was very excited about this new project:

'So, I found myself with this *Waverley* business! Captain Neill was in charge and he very much wanted me to stay with the project as I knew a lot of people who would be able to help us. Actually, Neill wanted me to be the Bristol and District Agent for the business. He had the foresight to see that the whole thing could be run quite profitably, and that with some hard work, it would be very successful, as well as enjoyable.

'The project lasted that six weeks and did very well but the *Waverley* had to move on. The *Balmoral* was still with us but it was obvious that it might have to be scrapped. We had one chap come all the way from Dundee to make an offer for it; he had the idea of using it as a floating restaurant - all we had to do was to take it to Dundee! We were pleased with this prospect as it might save the ship from being demolished.

'Mr Smith-Cox, Chairman of P & A Campbell, asked Captain Wide, the last Captain (he had been the Naval Officer in charge of some very secret goings on during the war) and myself to take it up for him. Captain Wide was not keen to take the ship up and I was even less keen, since it was in a frightful state. So, I didn't go. I can't remember who we managed to persuade to take it to Dundee. In fact, I did not even see the ship leave Avonmouth.

'The *Balmoral* needed a lot of money spent on it to even get it in a state to steam up north. By now it was winter and it would be a hard voyage. I wished the steamer's company a safe and happy journey but I just could bear to go to see them off. Amazingly, the crew did get it to Dundee and it was converted into a restaurant. For the first year, in fact, it was a success but the second year brought failure for the business and it seemed that the ship's fate was still in the balance.'

Tom knew that it could have gone either way then, but he had other ideas:

'Well, when I heard the news and the possible fate of the *Balmoral* I spoke to Captain Neill and he also thought it would be good to have it back and try and make it work. We had a bit of cash from various funds which could be used for its refit. The engines of the *Balmoral* were made by Newbury Engineering Company. They were two diesels and I knew they were extremely good runners. Anyway, we made sure that there were no debts with the ship and decided to have her back!

'The first problem was to find someone to bring it back from Dundee to Bristol, via the Clyde. I managed to get myself out of this, very decently. I just didn't want to do it. Captain Neill did manage to find another couple of chaps to go with him. I thought he was a brave man and didn't think too much more about it, knowing that I would see it on its return to Bristol. Well, it was winter and Christmas time before I heard another word about the little steamer.

'It was during Christmas lunch when the phone rang; Neill had called to let me know that they were having horrible weather where they were, around Cape Wrath. He said that he really thought this was it, but as he was such a leg-puller I didn't take him seriously. Well, apparently, she managed it to Glasgow for its refit. I wasn't really so indifferent to its plight or to Captain Neill's worries; I had kept in touch with the Coastguard to make sure that she wasn't in any real trouble.'

Tom is so very proud of this little ship:

'It was in 1986 when this little ship did its first trip from Bristol to Ilfracombe and, amazingly, it is still going to this day! It was a resounding success, this venture. She has just kept on going for all that time. The Chief Engineer, Andy Westmore, keeps the engines going year after year. He will continue to do so as long as we have the money to fund the project. Some people in Bristol who have had the experience of the *Balmoral*, say that they prefer it to the *Waverley*!

'The Captain we selected for the *Balmoral* was the Chief Officer from the *Waverley*. He really was a lovely, handsome chap, happily married with children. Sadly, for us, he was offered a job on the River Forth as a Pilot and we lost him a few years ago, as he wished to live closer to home.

'Actually the *Waverley* continued to come down for six to eight weeks from May each year, and then another week at the end of the season on her way back to Glasgow, where she lies up for winter. All the Charter Companies, the big charities and other firms who cruise on these steamers naturally prefer the *Waverley*.'

Tom has a story about one of the groups who hired the *Waverley* one evening:

'On one occasion, we had an interesting incident. It was during the last years that the ship was run by P & A Campbell, in the days when the *Balmoral* didn't do a lot of charters. A well-known national airline chartered the ship for an evening cruise out of Penarth. I didn't usually go on the evening cruises but on this trip the Captain particularly requested I was on board, as I knew more about aviators than he did. Well, we went down the river, it was a crisp, late Spring, early-Summer, evening.

'At that time of year, the visibility can change quite quickly in the Channel and unfortunately we ran into a cloud bank and ended up inching our way to Penarth pier by radar. These aviators and their wives and other guests came on board, the weather was deteriorating quickly and the cloud cover was building itself into a complete barrier. I think, to be fair, everybody was a little concerned by this stage. Our Captain, however, was not at all worried and said that it would be much clearer on the other side. So we phoned up Minehead, just to check, but they said that it was bad over there, too.

'We decided that the best course of action would be to anchor for a couple of hours to see if the cloud dissipated. These sort of manoeuvres which are not part of the trip are done very quietly so that the passengers do not become alarmed in any way. As it was, we must have made a jolly good job of covering up what we were up to as the passengers did not pay us any attention whatsoever! They were having such a jolly good time below, having a drink or two at the bar. At the conclusion of the cruise, the Senior Captain of this airline, who was with the party, and a couple of his mates, went on to the bridge to thank our Captain, and even said that one of their chaps had seen the Somerset Coast and a couple of cows! Well, it just shows you how people's imaginations can get them going. We had a jolly good laugh about it!

'The *Balmoral* made a rather epic voyage to Gloucester, once. You see, there was a lot of political trouble about getting this ship up to Gloucester, so during the winter of 1987 Captain Neill and I took a day off and went to see the Harbourmaster, Captain Boyak, at Sharpness and asked him how much clearance he could give me as we passed through the fifteen bridges between Sharpness and Gloucester. He said about 32 feet. Well, we knew that the *Balmoral* was about 31 feet-something, so we asked if he was certain about this. We eventually checked a couple of the bridges ourselves and they were about 33 or even 34 feet clear, so we were happy with the clearance that we would have through these bridges.

'We had the Lord Mayor of Gloucester waiting to be entertained at the Gloucester Docks and we had a lot of passengers who wanted to go on this epic voyage. The docks at Gloucester have little Dickensian shops and there is always a lovely atmosphere up there. Well, the trip started and a rather nasty gale blew up and although we had been told there would be a breeze, we were not expecting this!

'The Canal Pilot said that it wasn't going to be easy keeping the ship on the straight and narrow, along the canal. One particular bridge looked jolly narrow and as we were all concentrating on getting ourselves through the narrow entrance none of us spotted some very nasty, jagged pieces of iron that were just under the waterline.

'By now, the wind was pushing us on to the port side, straight over the iron, and we caught some of it on the bottom of the ship. Well, we were doing about 3 or 4 knots and the iron actually caught the plates that are placed together to make the hull. We had a lovely buffet laid out in the Main Saloon, on a lower deck, ready for our arrival in Gloucester, but water was pouring in on it. We went to our well rehearsed "Emergency Action Stations" and used the crew's mattresses to stop the flow of water, but the Lower Saloon could not now be used. So the food was moved to the Upper Saloon.

'Fortunately, that was the only, very narrow bridge that we had to go through. We arrived in Gloucester and decided to hold the ceremony in the Upper Dining Saloon, and said nothing about the little incident. We knew that they suspected something had happened as we had to get our underwater welders to work on the plates straight away! Then, because of all this activity going on we told them what had happened and they all had a jolly good laugh about it, really. Everyone wished us well and said how fine it was to have a ship in Gloucester.

'The gale carried on for the next couple of days, so we stayed there, and on the third day made our way back down the canal. After that, we realised that we should have looked out for any nasty little surprises, like the iron; it taught us a real lesson and we never took either of our ships up to Gloucester again.'

Not all the trips had happy endings, as Tom shows us with this little story:

'We had a rating on board the *Balmoral* who had been on board forever! The only time he had left the ship was during the short period when she was a restaurant ship at Dundee. He was just about the scruffiest sailor that I have ever met; during the war had been a Leading Seaman to start with but soon became de-rated to Able Seaman for various misdemeanours. He really was a bit of a scoundrel, and spent more time in Naval detention quarters than he did in seagoing ships.

'We used to spend our off-service day each week with the ship in Barry at that time, so he used to get the train back to Bristol. Well, the Superintendent of the GWR phoned Mr Smith-Cox, the Chairman of P & A Campbell, to speak to him about this rating. It seemed that the man had been travelling for a very long time without a ticket. Well, he was caught when a very thorough ticket inspector looked at the ticket that was offered him and saw it was a steamer ticket! Steamer tickets kept coming out of the man's pockets and the Ticket Inspector was definitely not impressed.

'When the rogue was brought before the Magistrates the Ticket Inspector told them that the chap was a 'human ticket machine.' It never happened again. How the chap managed to acquire so many tickets was because the Purser of the *Balmoral* liked to have as much assistance as possible in taking the passengers' tickets when they boarded at Ilfracombe, as it was always such a rush. The seaman was quite clever in some ways, as he just kept one of these steamer tickets as commission before returning the rest to the purser. He caught on to doing this at various destinations, so that he acquired a full complement of different coloured tickets, and could show the right coloured ticket on the train for that particular day. The purser, of course, had no idea this was going on, as it was impossible to check the very last passenger, and he would not have known that one was missing here and there. So our scoundrel managed to get away with it for a very long time. For all that, he was a super seaman.'

Tom still works with the *Waverley*:

'Waverley Excursions Limited, which was formed as a Charitable Trust in Scotland in 1969 and operated in the

Bristol area from 1981, has been very helpful to the Sea Cadet Corps and various Sailing and Yacht Clubs around the British Isles. We often take Cadets on the longer hauls that we still make and often an officer, a Chief Petty Officer or an Adult Qualified Instructor from one or other organisation, or the Sea Cadet Corps, sails with us; it is very good experience for them. We also carry young cadets from some of the sailing clubs so they can get some idea on what the conditions are like on a bigger vessel, and to show them how important it is to keep to the route that they take and to keep out of the way of other shipping, especially somewhere as busy as the Channel. I suppose what I really mean is that they see how disciplined it all is. We are always having to sail through some kind of a race that is going on and the yachts always keep well clear. However, there have been some nasty accidents where craft have got in the way of ships.

'Captain David Neill did such a tremendous amount to get this organisation off the ground and was probably one of the best navigators in the Channel. When we were offered the chance to get the *Waverley* up the River Avon to Bristol city, Neill was the chap to think it over and come up with the future plan. We discussed it with previous captains too, George Gunn from Swansea and Phil Power from Barry, and although we decided that it was slightly risky, at the end of the season, I believe in 1985, we had the offer of the use of a tug.

'We were counting on Ken Blacklock, the Chief Engineer, who was in all the briefings, as he had to give absolute immediate attention to the engine telegraph and any tele-graphic movements had to be undertaken straight away. So, the great day came. Other ships, such as the *Bristol Queen* had done it, but we knew that although she was longer, she had much more manoeuvrability. Luckily for us the ship went up perfectly; it was magnificent to watch.

'I waited at the Cumberland Basin and watched it go under the Clifton Suspension Bridge and we immediately decided to start trips up and down the river. Captain David Neill became more and more involved in the work. Unfortunately for us, he had to leave. Neill is now the captain of a modern, fairly large coaster.'

Tom went through a very low period of his life, when his first wife died but, true to this story, luck was always with him:

'I mentioned earlier that I left the Auxiliary Service because my wife had cancer. The work for the *Waverley* just got more and more, and I had been left on my own once Daphne had gone. Unashamedly, I thought that it was not much fun being on my own and luckily I had various affairs to help the loneliness. It didn't help much at all, but as luck would have it I was invited to the wedding of a chum of mine's daughter. I went along to Portbury Church and then to his house, in the garden of which there was a huge marquee with a lovely meal set out.

'I sat down at the table with a chum and his wife, Alec and Joan Birch, who had the other half of my house in Clevedon. Also, my dentist was at the same table, and a lady with a lovely hat. I thought she looked rather nice and as the meal proceeded I thought she looked even better. I was informed that the lady was a wealthy, titled widow with no children of school age. We all got up from the meal for a bit of dancing but I actually went up to her and invited her to have a drink with me at The Black Horse in Clapton-in-Gordano. She accepted my offer and we left the wedding for a while, had a little kiss on the way back and then went back to the dancing. We parted for a while as she went back to her daughter's flat in Bristol and I had to go back to work with the *Waverley* but we met from time to time and after a while, in 1984, got married.

'We moved from Edgehill Road down to Edgarley court as the house was far too big for us. The move was a great success, as I can see Clevedon Pier from our garden and can watch the *Balmoral* and *Waverley* on the river. I dip the Ensign from the mast in the garden as they go by.

'I moved into the house in 1983 but it was not until 1988 that the Pier could be used again. It was a great feat for the Trustees that they managed to get it done under all the appalling circumstances. When it is finished the *Waverley* should be able to go alongside the stone Pier, and we may well do it again, once the dredging is done. '

The final word in this tale, which I hope you have all enjoyed, falls to Tom:

'Well, what next? As I look back over my eighty-six years I wonder if I would have been better off following in my grandfather's footsteps. I think I can safely say no. There have been many ups and downs but it is good not to have your own way all the time, it makes you a decent, good-living, Christian person.

'I am no great pinnacle of virtue but I do basically try and lead a decent life and I do still go to church on Sunday, as I have for most of my life, but not all the time. I can still see the Captain of the *Breconshire*, before we met up with the Italians, reading us a prayer. Mercifully we did get away with that one and many more, so maybe the One Above does listen to what we say.

'Don't let me mislead you, I am not a religious fanatic, but I hope that after you have read this you will understand what I mean.'

*

Peninsular and Oriental Steam Navigation Company. Tom Under Five Naval Flags. Appendix 1

Passenger Ships	Rank Held Aboard Ship	Captain	Notes
RMS Strathnaver	Junior Assistant Purser July 1937 to January 1938.	Captain E.P. Lyndon. RANR.	Requisitioned 7 January 1940 as a Troop Transporter.
RMS Stratheden	Junior Assistant Purser May 1938 to September 1938.	Commodore Sir Richard Harrison RNR.	Requisitioned 19 March 1940 as a Troop Transporter.
RMS Rawalpindi	Junior Assistant Purser October 1938 to February 1939.	Captain M. Draper RNR.	Requisitioned 26 August 1939 as an Armed Merchant Cruiser. Became HMS Rawalpindi, sunk 23 November 1939 by German Cruisers Scharnhorst and Gneisenau when on Northern Patrol.

Royal Navy.

Ships	Rank Held Aboard Ship	Captain	Notes
HMS Mersey	Sub-Lieutenant RNR December 1939 to October 1940.	Commodore R.P Galer RNR.	
HMS Salopian	Sub-Lieutenant RNR October 1940 to May 1941.	Captain Sir John Alleyn RN.	Armed Merchant Cruiser, formerly MV Shropshire. Torpedoed and sunk in May 1941.
HMS Breconshire	Sub-Lieutenant RNR August 1941 to March 1942.	Captain C.A.G. Hutcheson RN.	Requisitioned November 1939 as Stores Carrier. Declared Constructive Total Loss 26 March 1942.
HMS Bulolo	Lieutenant later Lieutenant Commander RNR February 1943 to December 1946.	Captain R.L. Hamer RN. Captain C.A. Kershaw RN. Captain A.A. Martin RNR. Captain J.H. Plumer RN.	Requisitioned September 1939 as an Armed Merchant Cruiser. Operated as Combined Operations Headquarters Ship.
HMS Anson	Lieutenant Commander RN December 1946 to November 1948.	Captain M. Eveleigh RN. Captain D. Orr-Ewing RN.	Battleship. Flagship of Training Squadron during Tom's time on board.
HMS Tyne	Lieutenant Commander RN December 1948 to May 1949.	Captain J. Lee-Barber RN.	Destroyer Depot Ship at Harwich.
HMS Woolwich	Lieutenant Commander RN June 1949 to September 1950.	Captain P.R. Pelly RN.	Destroyer Depot Ship at Harwich.
HMS Dodman Point	Lieutenant Commander RN November 1950 to December 1951.	Captain J. C. Stopford. RN.	Destroyer Depot Ship at Harwich.
HMS Fulmar	Lieutenant Commander RN January 1952 to January 1954.	Captain J.H. Lane RN. Captain J. Ievers RN.	Royal Naval Air Station (RNAS) Lossiemouth.
HMS Hornet	Lieutenant Commander RN January 1954 to April 1956.	Captain J. Hodges RN. Captain R.E. Grant RN.	Main Coastal Forces Main Base, Gosport.
HQ, Allied Forces, Mediterranean	Lieutenant Commander RN April 1956 to September 1958.	Vice-Admiral Sir St. John Tynwhitt RN. Vice-Admiral Sir Ballin I. Robertshaw RN.	Headquarters Allied Forces Mediterranean. NATO Malta. (HAFMED).
HMS Warrior	Lieutenant Commander RN December 1958 to February 1959.	Admiral Sir William F. Davies RN.	North Atlantic Treaty Organisation (NATO) HQ, Northwood.
HMS President	Lieutenant Commander RN March 1959 to July 1962.	Commodore R.W.F. Northcott RN. Commodore R. Hart RN.	Commodore, Naval Drafting, Haslemere.
Ghana Navy	Commander RN, later Commander Ghana Navy September 1962 to May 1970.	Brigadier: G. Davies-Scourfield. Head of BJSTT	British Joint Services Training Team. (BJSTT).
Imperial Ethiopian Navy	Commander Imperial Ethiopian Navy August 1970 to May 1975.	His Imperial Highness, Rear Admiral The Prince Alexander Desta.	
Royal Naval Auxiliary Service	Port Naval Auxiliary Officer May 1975 to December 1980.	Captain G. Andrewes RN.	

Landings controlled from HMS Bulolo during Tom Foden's time aboard (in chronological order)

"CLYDE- BUILT SHIP DIRECTED D-DAY LANDING"

Our Naval Corresepondent, Francis Southcott, who was in that classic combined operations Headquarters ship H.M.S Bulolo, in the Bay of Normandy, on D-Day wrote a history of her towards the end of June when she was still in the bay with her staff superintending the "Build Up" of the British Army.

On June 6th, D-Day for the invasion of the Continent of Europe, "H.M.S. Bulolo" Flagship of an assault force, part of the Eastern Task Force, arrived off the coast of Northern France at five in the morning, three quarters of an hour later she anchored about seven miles off the Normandy beaches, roughly between La Riviere and Le Hamel, or almost dead centre in the bay of the Seine. Here was an honoured and historic job to direct the landing first of the famous 50th Division (Northumbrian) Commanded by Major General D.A.H. Graham, D.S.O. M.C., who was onboard, and later the 7th Armoured Division (The "Desert Rats"), and other supporting troops, including the Guards. She was flying the Broad Pennant of Commodore C.E. Douglas-Pennant, C.B.E. D.S.C. R.N. Commanding the Assault Force.

Bulolo had led the Force into the Bay, overtaking during the previous night the almost countless components of small, medium and large craft that had battled so gallantly with the English Channel, which was not in its quietest mood. The big Infantry landing ships followed astern of her.

HER MISSION

As she anchored, with the Cruisers behind to do the heavy supporting bombardment, the Assault craft went by for the initial attack, timed for 7.35 a.m. Bulolo, well armed as she is, was not there to fire. Her mission was to carry the Naval and Military Force Commanders and their staffs, together with the RAF Officers, and through her internal organisation and channels of communication to be responsible for seeing not only htat the storming of the beaches was successfully carried out but also that consolidation followed without delay.

How brilliantly she and other H.Q. ships succeeded the World now knows. At 6.20 an Enemy 6" shore battery opened fire, with the Bulolo as the apparent target. Two shells narrowly missed the Forecastle Head, one whistling through the rigging and plunging into the sea a few yards from the port side. Ten minutes later we moved out position and five minutes after that more shells fell around the destroyers and rocket craft in the vicinity. Those enemy shore batteries were soon silenced but later in the day when the wind freshened enemy aircraft were diving around. On the following day shortly after six in the morning enemy aircraft commenced diving through low cloud on shipping generally. The twelve F.W. 190's made off, taking violent evasive action, but were met by heavy A.A. fire, and two were destroyed over the beaches. The pilot of one, a veritable young Nazi, baled out and tried to use his Tommy Gun. He was injured in landing, and captured.

CLASSIC PIONEER

The Bulolo remained in the bay for days. Commodore Douglas-Pennant had as his Chief of Staff Captain B I Robertshaw, O.B.E. The two were frequently onshore in the period the "Build-Up" of the armies in Normandy was at its height. Captain C.A. Kershaw, the old English Rugger International Scrum Half, was Captain of the ship, having taken over from Captain R.L. Hamer, D.S.O. in December 1943 and he brought the ship from India to the Mediterranean, where, as Flagship of Rear Admiral Trowbridge, controlled the Anzio landing, working with an American Task Force. The Bulolo is the Classic Pioneer as an H.Q. ship, and has taken part in all the landing excepting those at Madagascar and Salerno. She was the model for other ships doing similar work, not excluding those of the U.S. Forces.

Bulolo was Rear Admiral Burroughs's Flagship for the North African Landings and at Algiers took over the communications work for the Casablanca Conference.

She was then Rear Admiral Troubridge's Flagship at the Sicilian landing and then part of the Syracuse Assault Force, as Flagship.

Bulolo in Peace and War

Although, with few exceptions, the complement of Bulolo has changed almost completely during the past few months, we are all proud to have had the opportunity of serving in a ship with such an illustrious record. Here, then, is a brief account of Bulolo through peace and war.

Bulolo was built on the Clyde by Barclay, Curle and Company, of Glasgow, in 1937 - 38, for the Burns, Philip Line of Sydney. Engined by Kinkaid of Greenock. She was built as a luxury liner, and even her war camouflage and structural alterations fail to hide the beauty of her graceful lines. Her displacement is 9850 tons. She is reputed to have cost more per lineal yard in building than any other vessel built on the Clyde.

Bulolo the ship takes her name from a gold mining area and also a river in New Guinea.

She made her maiden voyage in September 1938, and thereafter embarked on her normal peacetime run as a luxury liner between Sydney- New Guinea- New Britain- New Zealand and other Pacific Islands.

On the outbreak of war in September 1939, Bulolo was taken over by the Admiralty and sailed from Sydney to Simonstown, at which latter port she hoisted the White Ensign for the first time, and fitted out as an Armed Merchant Cruiser. Her armament was quite impressive- seven 6 inch guns and two 3 inch A.A. guns, together with several close range weapons. Her first Captain was Captain Petrie, D.S.O., R.N. (later of Glen ship fame).

From January 1940 until April 1942, she was employed on convoy escort duties and patrols in the Atlantic, during which time she achieved the remarkable record of escorting over 400 ships without losing one. In 1940-1941, she steamed over 175,000 miles in the Atlantic.

In 1942, she was taken into dock and emerged as the first Combined Operations Headquarters ship in the world; the principal tasks of such a ship being to carry the Naval, Army and Air Force Commanders and their staffs, and, through her communications, integrate the whole of the assault, build-up and consolidation of a Combined Operation. How brilliantly Bulolo and her sister H.Q. ships did their job is abundantly clear from the wonderful results obtained from 1942 onwards.

Her first task in her new role was as Rear Admiral Burroughs flagship in the North African landings. In early 1943, she was at Casablanca for the conference, acting as communications H.Q. She wore the flag of Rear Admiral Troubridge in the Sicilian landings and later at Syracuse as flagship of his "Overseas Assault Force", and also at Anzio.

Bulolo returned to England to play her part in the Normandy landings; which she did in no uncertain manner, wearing the broad pendant of Commodore. C.E. Douglas Pennant, C.B.E., D.S.O., R.N., who was Flag Officer Commanding an Assault Force attached to the eastern task force. In these landings Bulolo had the honoured task of playing her part in the landing of the famous 50 Division and also of the 7th Armoured Division (the Desert Rats).

After her task off the Normandy beaches was completed, she refitted at Southampton for the part she was intended to play in the war in the Far East. She arrived on the East Indies Station in June 1945; Rangoon had fallen in May; Operation Zipper was being planned with the ultimate objective of capturing Singapore and with Bulolo as Main H.Q. ship. The war, however, ended a few weeks before D Day, and she ended her operational days pleasantly and placidly in carrying out the Zipper cruise. At the end of October, she ran an errand of mercy to Sourabaya, bringing back 530 women and children to Singapore.

And so, H.M.S. Bulolo is now on her way to pay off, refit as a luxury liner and once again, take up her true role in life. May the rest of her active life be confined to peaceful cruises in the Pacific.